Sermons for Lent & Easter

Sermons for

Lent &
Easter

Selections from
Concordia Pulpit
Resources

CONCORDIA PUBLISHING HOUSE · SAINT LOUIS

MORE SELECTIONS FROM CONCORDIA PULPIT RESOURCES

Sermons for Funerals, Weddings & Civil Holidays (15-5103)

Sermons for Feasts, Festivals & Occasions (15-5104)

Sermons for Advent and Christmas (15-5105)

Copyright © 2008 Concordia Publishing House
3558 S. Jefferson Ave., St. Louis, MO 63118-3968
1-800-325-3040 • www.cph.org

Unless otherwise noted, Scripture quotations are from The Holy Bible, English Standard Version®. Copyright © 2001 by Crossway Bibles, a publishing ministry of Good News Publishers, Wheaton, Illinois. Used by permission. All rights reserved.

Scripture quotations for the sermons on pp. 29–46 and those marked RSV are from the Revised Standard Version of the Bible, copyright 1952 © 1971 by the Division of Christian Education of the National Council of the Churches of Christ in the United States of America. Used by permission. All rights reserved.

Scripture quotations marked NKJV™ are taken from the New King James Version®. Copyright © 1982 by Thomas Nelson, Inc. Used by permission. All rights reserved.

Excerpt from THE NEW JERUSALEM BIBLE, copyright © 1973 by Darton, Longman & Todd, Ltd., and Doubleday and Company, Inc. Used by permission of the publisher.

Hymn texts with the abbreviation *LSB* are from *Lutheran Service Book*, copyright © 2006 Concordia Publishing House. All rights reserved.

Some material taken from *Lutheran Service Book: Altar Book*, copyright © 2006 Concordia Publishing House. All rights reserved.

Quotations marked *Luther's Small Catechism* are from *Luther's Small Catechism with Explanation*, copyright © 1986, 1991 Concordia Publishing House.

Quotations from the Lutheran Confessions in this publication are from *Concordia: The Lutheran Confessions*, second edition, copyright © 2006 Concordia Publishing House. All rights reserved.

Manufactured in the United States of America

Library of Congress Cataloging-in-Publication Data

Sermons for Lent and Easter : selections from Concordia pulpit resources.
     p. cm.
     ISBN 978-0-7586-1380-6
     1. Lent—Sermons. 2. Easter—Sermons. 3. Lutheran Church—Sermons.
     I. Concordia pulpit resources. II. Title.

BV85.S463 2008
252'.62—dc22

                                                       2007034383

Contents

The Mountains of Life

REV. RICHARD ANDERSEN

Ash Wednesday

The Spirit of Calvary's Climb

Mark 6:1–6, 16–21

James Montgomery was twice imprisoned, several times challenged in court, and many times momentarily defeated by life's problems. He found refuge in his home in Sheffield, England. In this place of solace, which he named The Mount, he penned the beloved hymn "Come to Calvary's Holy Mountain" (*LSB* 435). Just as home was, for him, the physical place where "the troubled, peace may find" (*LSB* 435:3), Mount Calvary is the place of spiritual comfort and encouragement for all who believe in Christ.

How do you meet the challenging mountains of life successfully? How do you climb them and master their rugged slopes and sheer escarpments? We shall look at a variety of mountains this Lent. Tonight we focus on developing the right spirit or attitude to climb these mountains. Jesus shows us the right attitude, and He instills this same spirit in us too. In true Calvary spirit, we climb these mountains beginning with prayer, filled with Christ's love, and confident because of His victory.

FAKE CLIMBERS

Jesus loves people, but He is not fooled by their antics. He knows that many prefer to avoid their mountains, not to mention avoiding His. He understands that when some people find life hard they cover up and make it look like they are climbing when they are not. Jesus, too, thought about letting "this cup pass" (Mt 26:39), but He didn't. He knew that God judges those who fake it.

Jesus used the unpleasant word *hypocrite*. The term comes from Greco-Roman theater and designates an actor who plays his part behind a false face, a mask. No wonder Jesus urges us to "beware of practicing [our] righteousness before other people in order to be seen by them" (Mt 6:1). We are to be real climbers in life, not merely actors; genuine, not simply make-believe Christians.

Remember Ananias and Sapphira (Acts 5:1–11)? Their pretended generosity brought quick judgment from God. They made it appear that they had given their all when they sold a piece of property and laid the proceeds at the apostles' feet. In reality they kept back part for themselves. There was nothing wrong with that, but there was something very wrong with deceitfully pretending they gave more than they had. Their fate reminds us that no impostors belong in the Body of Christ. The apostle Paul put it this way: "Do not be deceived: God is not mocked, for whatever one sows, that will he also reap. For the one who sows to his own flesh will from the flesh reap corruption" (Gal 6:7–8).

We also know that God in Christ endured mockery and shame. When Jesus hung on the cross many passed by and hurled insults at Him, shaking their heads and saying, "You who would destroy the temple and rebuild it in three days, save Yourself!" (Mt 27:40). In the same way, some, like the elders and teachers of the law who appeared to be very religious, mocked Jesus. "He saved others," they said; "He cannot save Himself. He is the King of Israel; let Him come down now from the cross, and we will believe in Him. He trusts in God; let God deliver Him now, if He desires Him" (Mt 27:42–43). But Jesus said, "Father, forgive them, for they know not what they do" (Lk 23:34).

Jesus endured all this suffering to pay for our sins. He made up for all the fake climbers of the world by climbing the mountain of our hypocrisy. He received the punishment we deserved, so that the Father might forgive us. When you and I feel remorse because we have allowed our sinful nature to guide our thoughts, words, and deeds, the cross of Christ on Calvary's mountain assures our hearts of His grace and empowers us to have the right spirit for climbing life's mountains.

TRUE CLIMBERS

The spirit of Calvary that Jesus gives begins with prayer. "When you pray," instructed our Lord, "you must not be like the hypocrites. For they love to stand and pray in the synagogues and at the street corners, that they may be seen by others. . . . But when you pray, go into your room and shut the door and pray to your Father who is in secret. And your Father who sees in secret will reward you" (Mt 6:5–6).

Remember that while fake climbers were mocking Jesus, He prayed. Psalm 22 was in His heart and on His lips. On the cross, Jesus spoke the psalm's opening words: "My God, My God, why have You forsaken Me?" (Mt 27:46). And in His heart He continued praying the psalm that asks God to come quickly, to deliver, to rescue and save. He prayed in confidence that God would not hide His face but would listen and answer His cry for help.

As you face real mountains that may seem insurmountable, begin with prayer. You know you have been forgiven because of Christ's cross. Now proceed to call upon Him to deliver and help you in your particular situation. That is the spirit of Calvary that Jesus gives.

Second, be filled with love. Jesus overcame His great apprehension in the Garden of Gethsemane with love that was determined to obey the Father and save mankind. When Jesus was arrested, He still made a final appeal to Judas, calling him to repentance as He asked, "Judas, would you betray the Son of Man with a kiss?" (Lk 22:48). When Peter cut off the right ear of the high priest's servant, Jesus acted in love to right the wrong done by His follower. No faith on the part of the servant Malchus was involved. Jesus acted in loving grace alone. This is the same spirit He gives to you and me through faith as we face the mountains of trouble and adversity. Here is the spirit He gives to help us make the climb: love that supplants hate, love that rights wrongs.

Keith Miller wrote an autobiographical account of his struggle with anxiety, frustration, and compulsive behavior.[1] He sought help. He found encouragement. He recalls seeing the dawn break over the mountains and asking God for forgiveness. He believed the words of the apostle Paul, "God's love has been poured into our hearts through the Holy Spirit who has been given to us" (Rom 5:5). A new attitude, a new spirit, overcame his anguish. Love poured in. By God's grace, Miller was filled with Jesus' spirit of Calvary, the spirit of love. What Jesus did enabled Miller to master the mountains in his life.

Jesus confidently endured the cross for the joy set before Him (Heb 12:2). We can be confident of final victory in Christ. As God gives you confidence in Christ's victory over sin, death, the devil, and all that drags you down, God will help you ascend life's mountains until He finally calls you home.

Here is the message for our ascent: Jesus has climbed the most difficult mountain of all for us. There is a radical difference between Calvary and the mountains we face in life. Jesus surmounted Calvary once for all, so that we would never have to climb that mountain of death for our sins. We never could have done it—we never could have suffered enough to make up for our sins. But the sinless Son of God gave His life as the priceless payment, the sacrifice that atoned for us all. You can now confront your own troublesome mountains with the assurance of Christ's victory on your behalf. You do not have to—and indeed could never—climb to pay for your sins; Christ has done that already. Atop Calvary, on that bloodied cross, Jesus put all mountains in true perspective. He reconciled God and mankind. Now in that state of reconciliation, we can master the other, smaller mountains of life by the Spirit He gives.

We do not go it alone in our mountain climbing. Christ goes with us, enabling and strengthening us. Two American teenage boys with cerebral palsy aspired to be athletes. They went with their coach to Mount Kilimanjaro in Africa and ran nearly to the snow-crowned top because their coach encouraged them along the way. So it is with God, who fortifies us for the journey. Christ has been there before, and now through the power and encouragement of His Word and Sacraments, He moves us up and over life's mountains.

As James Montgomery wrote in the hymn "Come to Calvary's Holy Mountain":

---

1   Keith J. Miller, *Sin: Overcoming the Ultimate Deadly Addiction* (San Francisco: Harper & Row, 1987).

They that drink shall live forever;
'Tis a soul-renewing flood.
God is faithful; God will never
Break His covenant of blood,
Signed when our Redeemer died,
Sealed when He was glorified. (*LSB* 435:4)

Tonight as you are marked with the ashes of repentance and assured of forgiveness by the Sacrament of Holy Communion, know that during this season of Lent Jesus will continue to fill you with His Spirit through Word and Sacrament, giving you the true spirit necessary for mountain climbing. He gives the spirit of prayer, the spirit of love, and the spirit of confidence. Come with us the next five Wednesdays to receive power to deal with the other mountains in Lent's rugged range: the Mount of Temptation, the Mount of Suffering, the Mount of Loyalty, the Mount of Sacrifice, and the Mount of Triumph. Make this Lent a mountaintop experience in your journey of life!

Lent 2

The Mount of Temptation

Mark 1:12–15

One moment, as Jesus was baptized in the Jordan, He experienced the exhilaration of hearing His Father's voice of approval from heaven and saw the Holy Spirit descending to Him as a dove. Next He was in the wilderness, lodging with wild beasts. This stark contrast characterizes contemporary life. We go quickly from emotional heights to distraught valleys. Martin Luther put it this way: "You build a cathedral one day, and the day after you discover the devil has built a chapel next door." This is part of the equation of the real world: a tension between good and evil mixed together, between God's power that helps us live and temptation to live by our own power apart from God. The first sign of sonship is the struggle to live consistently as a son or daughter of God.

Tonight we focus upon the way to master the Mount of Temptation. The solution comes through Christ, who overcame temptation on our behalf so that He might aid us in our trials. God's grace in Christ gives us spiritual dedication, a devotion to the Father, a commitment to living God's way. During Jesus' temptation in the wilderness with the beasts, God declared war on Satan's stronghold.

Jesus was devoted to His Father and so won the war. This devotion to God's will, the same devotion He instills in your heart, shows itself with God-given courage, with an awareness of God's ministering angels, and with trust in God's love.

God-Given Courage

The Russian author Leo Tolstoy describes four ways people face temptations. First, he says, some who are incredibly frightened simply get high on drugs or drink. Intoxication does not work, however, with temptation; it sweeps us into its clutches.

Second, he says, some give way to despair and useless despondency, refusing to move forward or backward. They sit on their hands, stunned, immovable. But such inertia does not help either. It paralyzes us so we become like dirty water sucked down an open drain.

Or, third, they may resent the necessity of making a choice and so harden their hearts to whatever is before them. They may accept whatever satanic offer is made, thinking, like Faust, that they can out-trick the devil. But no one who makes a pact with evil benefits. Compromise with temptation destroys, and it often destroys quickly.

Last, Tolstoy says, some stand up to the temptation with bold courage, enthusiastically embracing it as an opportunity to let God win. We can win only because Christ has already achieved the victory. At His Baptism, Christ was publicly declared the Son of God and anointed with the Spirit. Satan tempted Christ to misuse His power as the Son of God for selfish purposes. Christ, however, was faithful to the mission the Father sent Him to accomplish. He resisted the temptations, fasting and living on the Word of God instead of making stones into bread. Instead of foolishly testing the Father's care by throwing Himself off the pinnacle of the temple, Jesus saved Himself in order to give His life later on the cross as the sacrifice for the sin of the world. In place of worshiping the devil to receive the kingdoms of this world, Christ honored the Father alone in order to bring the kingdom of God to us. Christ conquered temptation for us, and the Father sent angels to minister to Him (Mk 1:13).

An Awareness of God's Ministering Angels

Mark does not tell the story of Jesus' temptation in as much detail as Matthew and Luke. He uses an economy of language—yet what a picture he presents! For forty days Jesus was in that barren, broiling region. Mark pictures Jesus' temptation as being among the wild beasts. These beasts, in addition to being real animals, perhaps also represented the presence of Satan, since elsewhere Scripture describes the devil in similar terms (as "a roaring lion" in 1 Pet 5:8; as a serpent in Gen 3:1 and

Rev 20:2; etc.). But these satanic beasts did not deter the Savior. He was single-minded in His devotion to do God's will, and He was aware that God could command angels to effect His will. In Gethsemane, too, Jesus knew He could call upon thousands of angels to help if needed (Mt 26:53).

Angels are God's messengers, often sent to announce or carry out God's will on earth. Ps 91:11–13 says, "For He will command His angels concerning you to guard you in all your ways. On their hands they will bear you up, lest you strike your foot against a stone. You will tread on the lion and the adder; the young lion and the serpent you will trample underfoot." Satan misused this Scripture passage as grounds for testing Jesus, but understood properly, it is a passage of great comfort for us.

Although you do not perceive them, God may very well command angels to care for you as you climb the Mount of Temptation. They help you as they carry out God's good and gracious will. The celestial messengers are not only "out of this world" but also within the world. Now that's something to get excited about! There are many biblical examples of God delivering His faithful followers by sending angels. Remember Peter? He was locked up in prison. Angels set him free. Now, we have no guarantee that God will do the same thing today for you or me, but He could, and He just might! And regardless of whether He uses angels, God will help you win through Christ. No enemy is stronger than the One who is on your side!

Trust in God's Love

Jesus mastered the Mount of Temptation for us. He was the very Son of God, who gave His life to ransom us from our sins. Since the Son of God Himself successfully resisted temptation, He is now able to help us sons and daughters of God successfully overcome temptation.

Abraham was commanded to take his son, his only son, Isaac, to Mount Moriah and sacrifice him there. The patriarch was torn between his love for God, who had blessed him so magnificently, and his love for his son. The alternatives seemed impossible to reconcile. How could he be faithful to God without sacrificing the very child God had promised would carry on his line? But Abraham trusted God's grace, so he loaded his donkey and brought his boy to the place, trusting that God could even raise the dead (Heb 11:19). He took out his knife and was ready to slay the boy, but God intervened. Abraham's love and faith were not wasted nor was Isaac's life taken. God Himself provided a ram as a substitute sacrifice (Gen 22:13). That ram was a harbinger of Christ, our substitute, who was sacrificed on the cross for our salvation.

Even when the alternatives seem bleak for you, God will provide. He who did not spare His only Son will also give you all things (Rom 8:32). With faith in Christ's victory for you, with an awareness that God may command angels to guard you, and with God-given courage, you can master the Mount of Temptation.

Lent 3

The Mount of Suffering

Mark 8:31–38

The disciples seemed not to comprehend the profound message: "[Jesus] began to teach them that the Son of Man must suffer many things and be rejected by the elders and the chief priests and the scribes and be killed, and after three days rise again" (Mk 8:31). They heard the words *suffer, be rejected, and be killed.* They were stunned and thus missed the Easter words *rise again.* We, too, often focus only on the negative, the here and now, while on the Mount of Suffering; therefore, we miss the Gospel message about the eventual outcome.

There are three aspects of Christ's prediction: the rebellion, the reason, and the response.

THE REBELLION

Peter couldn't believe his ears. He didn't want to hear it. His Lord would suffer and die? Never! The burly fisherman rebuked his Master. He meant well, but in a selfish sort of way. He was unwilling to hear all Jesus had to say. He rebelled against the idea of suffering.

His reaction was understandable. No one wants to suffer nor see those they love suffer. Sometimes we just block out the idea altogether. In her studies on death and dying, Elizabeth Kubler-Ross noted five stages that the terminally ill and those who love them often pass through. One stage is denial and another is anger. Both involve rebellion against suffering. We want pleasure and enjoyment in life. We may consider pain and suffering to be evil and without any good result or purpose.

God's Word tells us otherwise. The apostle Paul put it this way: "Suffering produces endurance, and endurance produces character, and character produces hope, and hope does not put us to shame, because God's love has been poured into our hearts through the Holy Spirit who has been given to us" (Rom 5:3–5). To rebel against the very idea of suffering is to rebel against the possibility that it may be God's way of bringing about something very good for us.

The greatest good was accomplished by Christ's suffering on the cross for our sins. Thank God that Jesus did not rebel against suffering. Instead, He submitted to excruciating pain as He suffered the penalty for our rebellion against God. Jesus knew that He had to suffer if He was to accomplish our salvation—there was no way around it. The God of justice required a payment for all our transgressions, a payment we are too poor to make. Only one person could offer a sufficient ransom for us: Jesus Christ, the sinless Son of God. Out of His great love for us, Jesus chose to save us despite our rebellion—but Jesus knew it would cost Him His life.

THE REASON

There is a specific reason suffering exists in the world today. The episode in the Garden of Eden tells us that sin is the cause of all suffering. St. Paul repeats the theme: "Sin came into the world through one man, and death through sin, and so death spread to all men because all sinned" (Rom 5:12). There is a definite connection between sin and suffering. God's Word says, "The wages of sin is death" (Rom 6:23).

Now, this does not necessarily mean that if you are suffering, it is because God is punishing you for a particular sin. That is the erroneous conclusion of Job's "friends," and God said they were wrong. We often suffer simply because we live in a sinful world. Our bodies are corrupted by original sin and so susceptible to sickness, pain, and death. Other people may bring suffering on us by their inconsiderate actions. Worry, anxiety, fear, excessive anger, and depression may afflict us because of our fallen nature.

But this is not the whole story on sin and suffering. I know a person who had a radical mastectomy. The doctors thought they removed all the cancer, but it metastasized to several other critical areas. When she was back in the hospital for what turned out to be the final time, her friends would come and lament that such a youthful, healthy-looking woman should suffer so. But she would dismiss her anguish and pain by saying, "Look at Jesus—He suffered the pain of us all. By His suffering and death, He made it possible for my suffering to end in eternal life. His suffering ended in resurrection, and by God's grace, so will mine!"

She connected the cross of her suffering to the cross of Jesus. Her cross was quite different, of course, because she was not making up for sin; only Jesus suffered to atone for sin, and that of the whole world. But she knew Jesus called His followers to bear their crosses just as He bore His. She knew that on His cross the love of God was revealed, her sin was removed, and eternal life was guaranteed for her. The cross of Jesus transformed her suffering into victory.

THE RESPONSE

How should you and I respond to suffering? Dr. Paul Tournier told how a friend did research on many leaders in history. He discovered that many had been orphans, such as Alexander the Great, Julius Caesar, George Washington, Napoleon, Hitler, Lenin, and Stalin. He concluded that these orphans responded to their suffering by developing an intense determination to succeed. Yet human striving to succeed apart from Christ does no good in the end. Although these men became famous (or infamous), all have now died. None have survived. Their accomplishments now lie on the trash heap of history. Jesus said that if you try to save your life, living apart from God, you will lose it (Mk 8:35).

But Jesus also said that if you lose your life for His sake and for the sake of the Gospel, you will find it (Mark 8:35). If you live by faith in Jesus Christ, giving your life in service to God, your life will have meaning and purpose. You will have true life, life that will never end. Jesus makes this possible. He helps us deny ourselves, take up our crosses, and follow Him.

When suffering befalls us, it does little good to deny it or rebel against it. Nor should you feel you must try to figure out the reason for it; often that is impossible, except for the general reason that there is sin in the world. We usually cannot fathom God's purposes in letting us suffer, except to know "that suffering produces endurance, and endurance produces character, and character produces hope" (Rom 5:3–4).

When you suffer, keep your eyes on the cross of Jesus. The mountain that seems impossible to you may be climbed by His grace. Suffering is an opportunity for us to be drawn into a closer relationship with Jesus, as we rely on Him for strength, comfort, and the hope of life eternal.

A Christian mountain climber attempting to scale one of the lofty summits in the Sierra fell. His athletic body was crippled for life. Friends asked why he hadn't prayed to God for healing. "I have," he answered.

"But God has not healed you," they responded.

"Yes, He did," the man replied. "I prayed hundreds if not thousands of times for the Lord to heal me, and He finally healed me . . . of the need to be healed. The Lord helped me discover a peace inside the pain."

This is a response of one who has climbed the Mount of Suffering and viewed his life from the perspective of the cross. The grace of God in Jesus Christ gave him peace despite his suffering. The forgiveness of sin and promise of everlasting life gave him a joy that surpassed his pain. He was determined to give the rest of his life in service to Christ, confident of Christ's promise that in doing so, he would find far more than he lost. May God instill a similar attitude in us all. Amen.

Lent 4

The Mount of Loyalty

John 2:13–22

Loyalty means being faithful to responsibilities, duties, or promises. People express loyalty in varying degrees toward many things. Think of loyal sports fans who follow their team, win or lose; friends who speak up for each other; or husbands and wives who remain faithful to their wedding promise to love and cherish each other.

All these people are climbing the Mount of Loyalty. Then there are many others who do not remain loyal; their perseverance and determination fade when they encounter trials or adversity.

Jesus expressed great loyalty to the Father and to His mission for our sake. His loyalty brought about our salvation and also serves as a model for us to follow by the power of the Spirit. Our text describes Jesus as loyal in three respects: by fulfilling the Law, by expressing righteous anger, and by restoring the temple.

By Fulfilling the Law

Although He was God's only Son, Jesus loyally followed God's Law and submitted Himself to it. He kept the Mosaic Law (which contains both Law and Gospel). He attended synagogue every Sabbath as all loyal members of the covenant people did. He made frequent trips to Jerusalem as was required of loyal Israelites who worshiped the God of Abraham, Isaac, and Jacob. In these and many other ways, Jesus expressed His loyalty to His Father.

When it was time for Passover, Jesus went up to Jerusalem. Male Israelites were expected to be present in Jerusalem at the three annual festivals (the other two being Pentecost and Tabernacles). To loyal worshipers, these three annual pilgrimages were not sightseeing trips; they were journeys to the very dwelling place of God on earth, where they appeared "before the Lord," entering His real presence.

Jesus' loyalty to His mission for our salvation finally led Him to the cross, where He laid down His life as our Passover, the Lamb of God who takes away the sin of the world. He suffered judgment that we might be acquitted. He endured the torment of death to give us eternal life. Through faith in Christ, God considers Christ's righteous loyalty to be our own. We are forgiven in His name!

When Augustus was emperor of the Roman Empire, he was approached by one of his soldiers who was involved in a lawsuit. The soldier asked him to appear in court on his behalf. Instead, the emperor was going to send a subordinate to speak for the soldier in court. But the soldier, rolling back his sleeve, revealed his scars and shouted, "When you were in danger at Actium, I fought for you myself and was ready to die for you." Caesar Augustus, remembering the soldier's loyalty, changed his mind and went to court himself to ensure that the soldier was acquitted.

Jesus is the good soldier who was loyal to His Father. His scars from the cross are the proof of His loyalty. Jesus fought against all the powers of this dark age that oppose the Father and threaten us as well. He gave His life to defeat our sins of rebellion against God. Because of Christ's loyalty, He has persuaded the Father to acquit you and me, to declare us innocent and forgiven.

By Expressing Righteous Anger

Our text reveals another aspect of our Lord's loyalty that we dare not forget. While He welcomes repentant sinners, He also stands solidly against every form of evil and takes action to destroy it.

When people came from afar to the temple for Passover, they could not bring with them their sacrificial animals. Merchants made them available for purchase. People had various types of currency, so money changers would exchange it into the one coinage acceptable for purchase of animals and for the temple tax. The priestly hierarchy arranged for all these transactions to take place in the temple itself, in the court of the Gentiles, a place of prayer, and, of course, they reaped a share of the profit.

In His holy zeal, Jesus upset their tables, spilled their wares, and drove them out with a whip. His righteous anger was an expression of love for God, for mankind who needed to come to the Father, and for what is right. His loyalty was anything but halfhearted or wishy-washy.

In our modern world, the trend is toward ethical permissiveness, sexual license, and moral laxity and indifference. We seem to have lost the capacity for righteous anger. Righteous anger rightly confronts the forces that dishonor God, subvert morality, degrade others, and corrupt people. At times we need to brandish the whip of indignation and protest against the forces that would undermine the home, the nation, and the moral order.

Today many marriages, friendships, and other relationships lack firm commitment and loyalty. But Jesus Christ stands as our perfect role model. We who believe in Him strive to emulate His undying loyalty and firm resolve to do what is right, no matter how unpopular or how dire the consequences. Loyalty demands that we vigorously oppose those forces that threaten our relationships.

By Restoring the Temple

Jesus fought against corruption in the temple to restore it to its original purpose as a house of prayer for all people. The temple was for worshiping God, not for making a profit. In restoring the temple, Jesus was also moved by love for you and me. He knew our sin separated us from the Father, and He earnestly desired to reconcile us to God. He had come to earth to remove the barriers between God and mankind. Communion with God could take place at the temple only if it was cleansed and restored for its original purpose. This Jesus did, so that loyal worshipers would continue to receive God's grace through their worship there.

It is distressing that in many homes today there is a lack of commitment to worship and, therefore, to God Himself. Faithfulness, like a defective sparkplug, sputters. Have we become so accustomed to the visual splendor of network television, movies, and the grandeur of concerts that worship seems dull by comparison? Could it be that we just want to be entertained in church? Let us remember the true purpose of worship: it is to enter the very real presence of God, who comes to us through the Word and Sacraments, bestowing forgiveness, new life, and salvation.

Christ continues to restore temples today. We who believe in Christ have the Holy Spirit dwelling in us; we are temples of the living God. Jesus comes to us today in worship through the Word and Sacraments. He cleanses us as temples of the Spirit, sanctifying us, renewing our faith and loyalty. You are showing true loyalty and faithfulness to Christ by being here today.

Jesus also uttered an amazing promise: He Himself would destroy the temple and raise it up again in three days. The words of Jesus shocked the authorities. It had taken forty-six years for Herod to carry out his magnificent additions and improvements of the temple grounds. How could it be torn down in one day and rebuilt in three? But Jesus was talking about the temple of His body. Later, Jesus would tell them that one greater than the temple was here (Mt 12:6). As the incarnate Son of God, as God made flesh, Jesus fulfilled God's purpose in dwelling in the temple among mankind to make His grace available. What the authorities missed, the disciples recalled later after He was raised from the dead.

Here Christ's thorough loyalty is fully demonstrated. The real temple of His body would be torn down by the nails of the cross, yet death would not end His life nor ours. As the author of life, He would rise again to share His resurrection life with us. The religious authorities made an attempt to destroy His body or temple, but Christ's resurrection thwarted them. His victory is our victory, as eternal life is ours through faith in Him!

Lent 5

The Mount of Sacrifice

John 3:14–21

Father Maximilian Kolbe, a Polish Franciscan priest, refused to give way to the terror of Adolf Hitler and his forces of darkness. He believed God would somehow
win. Imprisoned in Auschwitz for his opposition to the Nazis, Father Kolbe heard
the prison commandant order ten prisoners to die by starvation as a reprisal for the
escape of one prisoner. When the ten were collected together, Kolbe saw a pale,
quivering Polish army sergeant sobbing, "My wife and my children . . . my wife and
my children." Father Kolbe pushed forward through the rigid formation of prisoners watching the selection, past the security guards, right up to the commandant
himself. Eyeing him straight on, Kolbe said in impeccable German, "I wish to make
a request, please."

"What do you want?" sneered the officer.

"I want to die in the place of this prisoner," he said, pointing to the weeping
sergeant. "I have no children or wife."

The stunned prisoners thought both men would die, one for his weakness and
the other for his audacity, but instead the commandant snapped, "Request
granted." Father Kolbe ascended the Mount of Sacrifice in the noblest way, out of
faith in his Lord and Savior Jesus Christ. He gave himself for another, following the
example of Jesus Christ, who gave Himself for us all. He acted out the words of the
apostle John: "We love because He first loved us" (1 Jn 4:19).

What about us? Has the love of God in Christ empowered you and me to
climb the Mount of Sacrifice?

Tonight let us consider Christ Jesus' sacrifice of Himself, and how, moved by
what Christ has done for us, we offer ourselves in service to God.

CHRIST JESUS' SACRIFICE OF HIMSELF

Picture the background of our text. Nicodemus steals quietly across the still streets
in the bleakness of a solemn night to converse with Jesus about deep theological
truths. Rather than speaking impersonally about abstract ideas, Jesus questions His
visitor about his own spiritual condition. "Do you," Jesus asks, "just consider Me to
be a good teacher, or have you been born again into the kingdom of God through
faith in Me as your Savior?" Jesus explains to the puzzled Nicodemus that he must
be born again, from above, by the Holy Spirit. This special kind of supernatural

birth comes about only through an act of God. It takes place through "water and the Spirit" (Jn 3:5). Together with the water of Holy Baptism, God sends His Holy Spirit, giving faith in Christ, the forgiveness of sins, salvation, and eternal life. The baptized are made children of God, their heavenly Father; they are born again.

Without this new birth a person is unable either to see or enter the kingdom of God. Those born only in the natural manner inherit the sinful nature common to all flesh, which is at enmity with God and excluded from His kingdom of grace. Without the second birth, a person remains in this state, now and forever.

In the Old Testament, the Israelites had grumbled against God as they wandered in the desert. God in His anger sent poisonous snakes to punish them for their sin, since the snake is the symbol of Satan and represents rebellion against God. Yet God in His mercy also provided a means of salvation. He told Moses to lift up a bronze serpent high on a pole to provide healing for those Israelites who had been bitten. Those who had faith in the promise of God looked at the bronze serpent and were saved.

So also, Jesus says, He must be lifted up in sacrifice so that everyone who believes in Him may have eternal life. Sinless Jesus will be made a serpent; He will be made sin for us and be cursed as He bears the sin of the world. In this way, He will provide eternal healing for those who look to Him in faith. St. Paul says, "For by grace you have been saved through faith. And this is not your own doing; it is the gift of God" (Eph 2:8). Many make sacrifices for the wrong reasons, but Jesus made His sacrifice for the right one: in obedience to God the Father, out of love for humanity, He gave His life willingly and generously for the salvation of the world.

As you hear the message of Christ today, the Spirit is working in your heart, renewing your Baptism and granting forgiveness, new life, and strength for Christian living. This is going on right now! Like one of the Israelites in the desert, acknowledge that your life has been bitten by the poison of sin and that you can't save yourself. Then look to Jesus lifted high on the cross of Calvary, suffering for your sin to earn forgiveness for you. Believe that He died and rose for you. You are a new creation in Christ!

OUR SACRIFICE OF OURSELVES IN RESPONSE

"I appeal to you therefore, brothers, by the mercies of God, to present your bodies as a living sacrifice, holy and acceptable to God, which is your spiritual worship" (Rom 12:1). The sacrifice of Jesus Christ moves us to sacrifice ourselves in service. One aspect of our sacrifice is self-denial. Paul says, "We know that our old self was crucified with Him in order that the body of sin might be brought to nothing, so that we would no longer be enslaved to sin" (Rom 6:6). Every day we are to live out our Baptism by dying to sin and rising again to life for God.

We consecrate to God our minds, wills, hearts, ideas, plans, desires, and all our activities. Christ takes all our faculties, and since they are filled with sin, He puts them to death on the cross. He then gives us Himself in exchange: His own mind, will, heart, ideas, plans, and desires. Our old self is denied and Christ is affirmed. Through Baptism Christ brings us into His Body, the Church, and He places Himself in us through His Spirit. The action is all His.

A second aspect of sacrifice is serving others. Having been redeemed by Christ and renewed by the Holy Spirit, you and I now live in service to others, walking in the footsteps of Jesus. We do not do this to merit blessing, but only as an expression of our faith and confidence in Christ alone.

There is the true story of Kagawa, a young Japanese orphan who was taken into a strife-torn home. He had little hope for the future, but eventually he was able to go to school and began to learn English from an American missionary who also shared the Gospel with him. The love of Christ swept over Kagawa and gave him new life. He became one of the most influential Japanese Christians of all time. He could have risen to prominence in politics, literature, or business, but he gave all that up to spend his life sharing the love he found in Christ. He founded orphanages and homes for the elderly. He protested the beginnings of World War II, was arrested for it, and was threatened with death.

When the war was over, Emperor Hirohito went to visit Kagawa, the accused traitor who had served the lifted-up Christ. Even those outside the Christian community recognized Kagawa's contributions to society because he had established so many institutions to help the poor, the elderly, and the homeless. He climbed the Mount of Sacrifice, knowing that what he gave up was returned to him a thousandfold by the joy that comes with serving Christ.

If you are becoming lethargic in doing good works, if you feel like a marionette being moved by strings held in other people's hands, if you have lost heart and are just going through the motions, look again at Jesus Christ on the cross, conquering the Mount of Sacrifice. He did it for you. He forgives your failings and gives you a new heart as you are born again of water and the Spirit. God daily renews His baptismal grace in you and calls you today to live a little more for others than you did yesterday and to proclaim the love of Christ more powerfully through your service. May we all offer our lives to the praise and glory of Christ, who offered Himself on the Mount of Sacrifice for our salvation!

Lent 6

The Mount of Triumph

John 12:20–33

THE DILEMMA

I have never met a person who planned on failing at an endeavor or falling short of their goals. We may not always achieve what we want, but the plan is never to be a failure. For example, ask parents whose kids have run into trouble with the law or with drugs if they planned on their kids turning out that way, and they will emphatically say no. Did the man who just lost his job because of a corporate takeover plan on being unemployed at age 50 with kids in college? Of course not! People desire to achieve, to succeed, to reach the top in triumph, whether in sports, academics, business, or marriage. The problem is that often we cannot, or do not, achieve what we want in life.

PEOPLE SEEK TRIUMPH THROUGH MANY MEANS

There is a great variety of strategies and methods people employ to achieve success. Some have suggested that the strategy for triumph in life is taught in kindergarten: share your possessions, play fair, don't hit people, put things back where you found them, and clean up your own mess.[2] These rules provide a simple, workable strategy for the early stages of life and, some suggest, guarantee success for adults as well. Yet climbing the Mount of Triumph despite life's trials, failures, and suffering requires more than just washing your hands before you eat or taking a nap every afternoon.

Others promote more sophisticated strategies. One pastor and best-selling author asserts that the deepest needs in every human are for self-esteem, self-worth, and personal dignity.[3] This pastor argues that for churches to prosper and grow, they should proclaim a message that affirms the personal worth of every person. Churches should talk about how great we are going to become as we make the effort to walk with Christ in triumph throughout this life. Success comes through our own efforts to think positively and live a Christian lifestyle. The amazing per-

---

2 Robert Fulghum, *All I Really Need to Know I Learned in Kindergarten* (New York: Random House, 1988).

3 Robert H. Schuller, *Self-Esteem: The New Reformation* (New York: Jove Books, 1985).

sonal success of this pastor and the size and prosperity of his church are offered as proof that this formula does in fact result in triumph.

THE GREEKS

The Greeks in our text who wished to see Jesus knew all about self-help religions. Their Hellenistic culture was full of religions and philosophies that promised success in life through rituals, secret knowledge, membership in exclusive organizations, and maintaining certain lifestyles. These Greeks had been exposed to all these methods, and perhaps they had even tried some of them. But now they had reached the conclusion that it was all futile. They knew that all human efforts to please God and win His favor are doomed to failure because of our sin. No matter how hard we try, how sincere we are, how smart we may be, or how much success we may achieve, it is inevitable that we will have disappointments, meet with failure, suffer, and eventually die. So they took a completely different direction: they wished to see Jesus.

Our text leaves us in suspense, for it does not explicitly tell us whether they were able to see Jesus. During His earthly ministry, our Lord displayed some reluctance to interact with Gentiles because His primary mission was to the lost sheep of Israel (Mt 15:24). Yet Jesus was soon to die for the sins of all, Jew and Gentile alike, and in our text He describes how after He is lifted up, He will draw all people to Himself (Jn 12:32). Jesus' response to the request of the Greeks, though perhaps not directly spoken to them, certainly speaks to their concerns and is recorded in Scripture for the benefit of us as well.

The coming of the Greeks indicated that Jesus' hour had come (v. 23); it was time for Him to be glorified as He gave His life for the salvation of all. Jesus had mixed emotions. The thought of bearing the punishment for the world's sin caused Jesus distress, but it was for this express purpose that He had come into the world (v. 27). The Father spoke to Him, assuring Him of triumph and glory, but Jesus said that the heavenly voice was more for our benefit than His (vv. 28–30). The Father's words point us to Jesus as the one who would be triumphantly glorified. If we seek triumph, we must seek it through Christ.

CHRIST'S RECIPE FOR TRIUMPH

Jesus described His strategy for triumph using a simple, earthly analogy: "Truly, truly, I say to you, unless a grain of wheat falls into the earth and dies, it remains alone; but if it dies, it bears much fruit. Whoever loves his life loses it, and whoever hates his life in this world will keep it for eternal life" (vv. 24–25). The farmer who hopes for a harvest must first plant the seed into the ground. There it "dies," buried in the earth. But later it springs forth with new life, yielding an abundant harvest, providing life for many other plants and for people as well.

This miracle of nature points to the miracle of Christ's own resurrection. If Christ had given in to the temptations of the devil and sought triumph in worldly terms, seeking fame and fortune instead of death on a cross, He actually would have been a failure. He would not have completed the mission the Father entrusted to Him.

But Christ was faithful to the Father's will. He spent His life in humble service, fatally offering His life on the cross as the payment for the sin of the world. His ignominious death appeared on the surface to be His defeat and the triumph of the devil. But Christ knew that through His obedience and submission to death, He would be glorified; the glories of heaven that were His from eternity would be restored to Him, and He would be proclaimed King of kings and Lord of lords. And not only was Christ raised again to new life, but His death also has resulted in new life for millions who believe in Him. The death of the one Jesus Christ has yielded a rich harvest of many souls to eternal life.

This same miracle of life through death, glory through humility, and triumph through apparent defeat also occurs in the lives of Christians. In the paradox of God's kingdom, we live and triumph only if we first die.

God's Law serves as a mirror of our thoughts, words, and deeds, showing our imperfections, revealing what in us needs to die. We are baptized into Christ's death, but we are also baptized into Christ's resurrection. While the Law makes us die to sin, the Gospel raises us up with new life, eternal life. God is killing and giving new life even now as you hear His Word proclaimed.

Glory comes through humble service. Christ says, "If anyone serves Me, he must follow Me; and where I am, there will My servant be also. If anyone serves Me, the Father will honor him" (v. 26). The lives of Christians are often quite ordinary and routine. There may not appear to be anything glorious about our lives. We may have just as many problems in life as others, or even more. We may suffer, become discouraged, and experience setbacks. Jesus never promises otherwise—we cannot expect any more worldly success than He Himself had. But Jesus does promise us that by following Him in humble service, living by faith in Him, one day we will end up where He is—in glory everlasting. We who honor the Son here on earth will one day be honored by the Father in heaven. Because of Christ's triumph on the cross, we who die with Him will rise again in triumph!

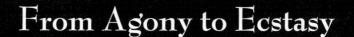

From Agony to Ecstasy

Rev. Paul G. Lessmann

Author's note: From agony to ecstasy: blood, sweat, and tears; heart, hands, and voices. These are the theme and titles of this midweek Lenten series, which is somewhat unique, I believe. The series talks about some very ordinary experiences and ingredients in our Lord's Passion and in human life: blood, sweat, tears; heart, hands, and voices. The series attempts to demonstrate how the agonies of our Lord produced the great ecstasies of our faith.

Editor's note: These sermons make use of the Revised Standard Version of Holy Scripture.

Ash Wednesday
Blood Will Tell

On May 13, 1940, toward the beginning of World War II, just three days after he had become leader of the British national coalition government, Winston Churchill made a celebrated speech to the Commons. He said, "I have nothing to offer but blood, toil, tears, and sweat." Later, at Dunkirk, he said, "We shall go on to the end, whatever the cost may be."

Those famous, daring statements of determination helped to win the war. They also well describe what Christ, our Lord, went through for us to win the war against sin and Satan. It was blood, sweat, and tears—and heart and hands and voices. Tonight it is blood.

> Glory be to Jesus,
> Who in bitter pains
> Poured for me the lifeblood
> From His sacred veins! (*LSB* 433:1)

I hope you notice how often blood is mentioned in the hymns we are singing tonight—and then remember that we are actually receiving the body and blood of Christ in the Eucharist that follows.

Blood will tell! When you go to a doctor's office and a technician draws a sample of blood from your arm, it is amazing how that sample of blood talks. It talks about corpuscles, cholesterol, sugar, disease, and many other things—both good and bad.

Blood talks! When Cain killed his brother Abel, God confronted Cain and said, "What have you done? The voice of your brother's blood is crying to Me from the ground" (Gen 4:10).

Blood will tell. The blood that runs in your veins tells a lot about who you are, who your parents and grandparents are. If your name is Jones, you're probably going to be something like your parents, whose name is also Jones—not completely, but somewhat. Blood will tell!

Blood gives life, health, and salvation. Just think how many lives have been saved by blood transfusions. It is important that we donate our blood to blood banks. Blood transfusions give life.

One of the most unusual passages in the Bible is the Lord's instruction to Moses to tell the people, "The life of the flesh is in the blood; and I have given it for you upon the altar to make atonement for your souls; for it is the blood that makes atonement, by reason of the life" (Lev 17:11). While we may not fully understand this passage, it is saying that the vitality—the life force—is in the bloodstream of every living creature. This is why the Israelites were instructed to paint the lintel and doorposts of their houses with the blood of the Passover lamb when they were in slavery in Egypt. Because of the blood, the angel of the Lord passed over that house, and the life of the firstborn within that house was spared. This, too, is why priests of the Israelites would sprinkle blood on the altar in the temple and why Moses in Exodus 24 took a basin of blood and threw half of it on the altar and the other half on the people. It was the blood of an animal in place of the blood of the people. Along with the shedding of that blood, the people were forgiven and saved.

How would you like it if God had instructed me to tell you that the only way you could receive forgiveness for your sins, the only way you could have a right relationship with God, the only way you could have peace with Him, and the only way you could go to heaven would be if I took a basin of blood and threw it out over you every time we came together to worship?

I have good news for you. We don't have to do that. That's what Lent is all about. St. John says, "The blood of Jesus, [God's] Son, cleanses us from all sin" (1 Jn 1:7). Once and for all and forever. Jesus poured out His lifeblood so that we may have forgiveness and life by and with Him. "For our sake He made Him to be sin who knew no sin, so that in Him we might become the righteousness of God" (2 Cor 5:21). Every time you look at the cross, remember that glorious fact. We simply trust and His righteousness is ours.

So now we are blood brothers—Jesus and you and I. When I was a boy, we had our clubs. And in one of those clubs, it was necessary for each of us to prick our fingers with a pin and then mix our blood together. I wouldn't advise that nowadays with a lot of awful diseases going around, but at the time, the ritual made us blood brothers.

We are blood brothers with Jesus. It was His blood for our blood. And His blood tells us that God is our Father, and we are His children. It cost Jesus plenty— His lifeblood.

That's the agony of the Passion. Jesus suffered, shed His blood, and died. Our agony and ecstasy is this, as St. John says: "If we say we have no sin, we deceive ourselves, and the truth is not in us" (1 Jn 1:8)—that's agony. But "if we confess our sins, [God] is faithful and just, and will forgive our sins and cleanse us from all unrighteousness," for "the blood of Jesus, His Son, cleanses us from all sins" (1 Jn 1:9, 7). That's ecstasy.

> Jesus, Thy blood and righteousness
> My beauty are, my glorious dress;
> Midst flaming worlds, in these arrayed,
> With joy shall I lift up my head. (*LSB* 563:1)

Lent 2

Sweating It Out

You've got to sweat it out! It takes sweat to work out life and salvation! Let me refresh your memories on our Lenten series theme. We're talking about blood, sweat, and tears; heart and hands and voices. All of these are connected with the Passion of our Lord Jesus Christ, who died on a cross for you.

Last week it was blood, the real essence of the Passion. Jesus shed His blood for you! Tonight it is sweat. Jesus "sweated it out" for you!

We all know what it means to sweat. Often there's real agony connected with sweating—or shall we say that the agony and energy of what we're doing causes sweat to exude from our pores.

Our Lord Jesus Christ, God's only Son, came down from the heavens to be like us in all things, including this very human experience of sweating. Tonight we find Him on the Mount of Olives, in the Garden of Gethsemane, a stone's throw away from His disciples. He kneels down on the hard ground to pray. His flesh and blood do not really want to face the agonies of the crucifixion, which He knows lies before Him. And so, anxiously, He prays: "Father, if Thou art willing, remove this cup from Me; nevertheless not My will, but Thine, be done" (Lk 22:42). This is where our first text comes in (Lk 22:44): "Being in an agony He prayed more earnestly; and His sweat became like great drops of blood falling down upon the ground." He was really sweating it out!

My other primary text is from the Old Testament, right at the beginning of human history. Adam and Eve had just disobeyed God and fallen into sin. God placed a curse upon the serpent, then talked about the pain the woman would suffer as a result of this sin. Then God turned to Adam and said, "Cursed is the ground because of you. . . . In the sweat of your face you shall eat bread, till you return to the ground, for out of it you were taken; you are dust, and to dust you shall return" (Gen 3:17, 19).

Both of these texts speak of sweat, quite obviously. Did you know that the word *sweat* is used only one other time in all of Scripture? That's in the book of Ezekiel (44:18) where the Lord God tells Ezekiel that in the "temple" of heaven, the priests who minister before the Lord will wear only linen garments. They will not wear wool or anything that causes sweat. There's nothing wrong with sweat, of course. It often comes from hard work. But in heaven, the time for sweaty, difficult labor will be over. There our service of God will be pure joy.

The Sweat of Life

While life can be beautiful—and that's how God intended it to be—don't ever get the idea that "life is just a bowl of cherries" or that life is easy. Although we often glibly use the expression "no sweat," it takes hard work and sweat to lead a meaningful and productive life.

God said to Adam, "In the sweat of your face you shall eat bread." There are all kinds of sweat in life.

There is the sweat of hard work to earn a living and support a family. If you young people don't know what that is, ask Mom and Dad. There are thorns and thistles and alligators out there, making our life's work difficult. And sometimes when there's sweat, there's also pain—aching joints, aching backs, tired bodies.

There is also the sweat that is so uncomfortable for all of us in the terrible heat of summer.

We sometimes have to "sweat it out" when we didn't do our homework or did something wrong.

And who of us doesn't know all about "sweaty palms" when we're anxious or nervous, writing a test at school, or when we feel self-conscious and ill at ease among strange people?

And then there is that awful cold sweat that hits us once in a while when we're afraid or in some kind of crisis.

Yes, we all know about sweat. Our Lord said about every one of us, "In the sweat of your face you shall eat bread." You've got to sweat it out. It takes sweat to work out life.

The Sweat of Our Lord

It took sweat for our Lord Jesus Christ to work out our salvation! Don't ever get the idea that just because He was the Son of God it was an easy thing for Jesus to suffer and die for our salvation. Remember, Christmas tells us that Jesus became flesh and blood just like us. Now we see Him praying to His heavenly Father. There was nothing unusual about that. He did that all the time—and we might learn something from that. But this was the only time, as far as we know, that He reasoned with His heavenly Father. "Father, I'm not so sure I want to suffer that awful crucifixion that lies ahead and die like a common criminal. Couldn't You find a better way to reconcile the world to Yourself?" And He wrestled in prayer with His heavenly Father so anxiously, so persistently, that "His sweat became like great drops of blood falling to the ground." But He added the words, as we all should when we pray, "Nevertheless not My will, but Thine, be done" (Lk 22:42).

Have you ever stopped to think what this world and our lives would be like if the understandable human anxiety of Jesus had prevailed over His determination to fulfill His Father's will? What if the Father had taken that awful cup of suffering away from Jesus? What if His crucifixion had not taken place?

Our all-wise heavenly Father, who hears and answers all our prayers, saw fit to make His Son, Jesus, go through the suffering that lay ahead. He did not take the cup away. That was the agony and the sweat of Gethsemane. But the ecstasy is this: "There appeared to Him an angel from heaven, strengthening Him" (Lk 22:43), so that He could go on—despite the blood, sweat, and tears—to work out our salvation and gain for us peace with God.

This is our great ecstasy in life and in eternity: because Jesus "sweated it out" for us, God the Father has given us the free gift of salvation. As we continue in faith, strengthened not by an angel but by God's Word and Sacrament, we can be sure that Jesus, our brother, is with us every moment of every day.

WE NEED TO SWEAT IT OUT

But don't ever get the idea that just because Jesus sweated it out for you and me, the rest of our days on earth as baptized Christians are going to be no sweat at all. Although salvation is a free gift from God, it takes some honest sweat to remain a Christian, to work out our life and salvation. St. Paul said in our third text, "Work out your own salvation with fear and trembling; for God is at work in you, both to will and to work for His good pleasure" (Phil 2:12–13).

When you are in a cold sweat about some crisis that you face, when you are sweating out some difficult situation, when you have sweaty palms because you are anxious and nervous, has it ever occurred to you to "take it to the Lord in prayer" as Jesus did? And when you pray, is it with the same intensity shown by Jesus, who sweated as if great drops of His blood were falling on the ground? Do you, like Him, pray that the answer be according to the good and gracious will of your heavenly Father? Do you realize that Jesus is right there with you all the while, sweating it out with you, praying for and with you, and strengthening you, even as an angel strengthened Him?

Yes, it takes work, hard work, to remain a Christian! The Holy Spirit works in us through Word and Sacraments to keep us steadfast in the faith. With the Spirit at work in us, we work and sweat to live a morally decent Christian life: to put God first in our life; to use His name in prayer and thanksgiving day after day and definitely not to curse or otherwise use His name in vain; to worship Him, read His Word, and receive His Holy Supper often; to be obedient children and worthy Christian parents; to make marriage honorable and not to take the privileges of marriage before or outside of marriage, no matter what the rest of the world does; to be protective of human life from conception to grave; to be honest in our business dealings; to avoid slandering or gossiping about our neighbor; to be content with what the Lord has given us and not to covet what others have. I say this takes work—hard work—as we work out our salvation with fear and trembling.

And it takes work to share our faith with others, to serve our Lord with gladness within the Christian congregation, to live as a Christian in our community and world. Someone has said, "It isn't enough for Jesus to come to you; you also must go somewhere with Him."

Jesus certainly sweated it out for us. Let's ask the Holy Spirit to help us day by day to "sweat it out for Jesus."

Lent 3

His Tears, Our Tears, No Tears

John 11:35; Luke 19:41–42; Psalm 56:8; Revelation 21:4

If you attended our first two midweek Lenten services, by now you know it cost our Savior plenty to work out our salvation, to buy each and every one of us back for our God, to make us forgiven children of our heavenly Father. It took blood, sweat, and tears; heart and hands and voices. As a result, we go from "agony to ecstasy."

On Ash Wednesday we talked about blood. He shed His blood for us. Last week it was sweat. He sweated it out for us! Tonight it is tears: His tears, our tears, no tears.

Tears and weeping are mentioned so frequently in the Bible that it would be difficult to count just how often. Here are four examples—and these are my texts:

Jn 11:35: Jesus wept.

Lk 19:41: When He drew near and saw the city He wept over it.

Ps 56:8: Put Thou my tears in Thy bottle.

Rev 21:4: [God] will wipe every tear from their eyes.

His Tears

Perhaps you have never thought about it, so think about it now. In your wildest imagination, have you ever thought that God could or would cry? That He would actually shed bitter tears? That's totally contrary to common images of God as

33

macho or aloof. Would a strong man such as Hercules or Atlas or Superman or Rambo break down and cry? Would the God who mightily made the entire universe be capable of crying like a baby?

Well, the answer is yes. In Genesis 6, when "the Lord saw that the wickedness of man was great in the earth . . . [He] was sorry that He had made man . . . and it grieved Him to His heart. So the Lord said, "I will blot out . . . man and beast, creeping things and birds of the air, for I am sorry that I have made them' " (Gen 6:5–6). While He spared Noah and His family, God was angry and hurt enough to, we might say, shed enough tears to flood and destroy the entire world of that time.

But tonight as we approach the midpoint of our Lenten season, we're much more interested in the fact that God, in the person of Jesus, really wept. Scripture says point-blank that twice, shortly before His Passion, the mighty Son of God actually cried.

One of those is the shortest verse in the Bible, Jn 11:35: "Jesus wept." The occasion was four days after the death of His good friend, Lazarus, the brother of Mary and Martha. As He stood at the grave of His dear friend and saw Mary and Martha weeping over the death of their brother, Jesus broke down and cried with His friends. Why did He cry when He knew He was going to bring His friend back to life? Was it in sympathy for Martha and Mary, seeing them so sad in the agony of separation from their brother? Was it out of sorrow for Lazarus, whose illness and suffering had culminated in death? Or was it in sympathy for Lazarus, who now would have to return to the pains of life on earth? We don't really know, but it's something to think about!

The other time Jesus wept was on Palm Sunday, the beginning of Holy Week. Jesus had just begun to approach the city of Jerusalem in that remarkable Palm Sunday procession. His disciples and the crowds had cheered Him with the words, "Blessed is the King who comes in the name of the Lord." The Pharisees didn't like that, and they said, "Teacher, rebuke Your disciples." To that He replied, "I tell you, if these were silent, the very stones would cry out" (Lk 19:38–40). And now the words of our second text: "When He drew near and saw the city, He wept over it, saying, 'Would that even today you knew the things that make for peace! But now are they hid from your eyes' " (Lk 19:41–42).

Why do you think Jesus wept over Jerusalem? It may have been that He saw most of the inhabitants having a good time, while the poor were starving in their midst. Or perhaps it was that the inhabitants had become as corrupt as those of Sodom and Gomorrah—or modern America, if you will—many of them high on alcohol or drugs or living in sexual immorality. But I'm sure that the greatest reason for His tears was that they were neglecting the things that belonged to their peace: they were neglecting and even opposing Him, the Christ, the great peacebringer. And that sin of unbelief, that lack of faith in Jesus Christ, is the greatest sin of all. Jesus knew that the terrible destruction of Jerusalem would take place in forty years—so He wept!

Is there anything in your life right now that would cause Jesus to weep about you? Of course there is—and in mine too. Jesus went to the cross to save us from those sins. Now He expects us to overcome such sins more and more with the help and power of the Holy Spirit. When we are tempted, He expects us to ask Joseph's question: "How . . . can I do this great wickedness, and sin against God?" (Gen 39:9).

OUR TEARS

Jesus wept! Never forget it! And we cry too—from the moment of our birth, through the many scrapes and sadnesses and frustrations of living, down to the final agony of our death.

Never be ashamed to cry! Don't ever believe that "big girls don't cry" or that it's a "sissy weakness" for men to cry. Remember that Jesus, too, cried when Lazarus died. God made us able to cry. Sometimes that is the healthiest release and relief for our grief.

Jesus came to this world to have experiences like ours in all things (but without sin)—including weeping. He knows all about our tears of anguish and anger; of hurt and heaviness; of deprivation, desperation, and despair.

And those tears mean much to Him! You may pour out your tears with your fears when you pray. In 2 Kings 20, godly King Hezekiah cried bitterly as he prayed for the healing of his disease and for prolonged life. God saw those tears, healed him, and extended his life fifteen years.

In Psalm 56:2, King David was complaining and praying, "My enemies trample upon me all day long." And then he spoke some very strange-sounding words to the Lord (v. 8): "Thou hast kept count of my tossings; put Thou my tears in Thy bottle! Are they not in Thy book?"

Our tears are recorded in God's book! Our tears are in God's bottle! I'll bet you never heard of tears in a bottle. How would you like to try collecting your tears—or those of someone else—and put them in a bottle? Well, in ancient days sometimes a narrow-necked bottle called a *lachrymatory* was found in a tomb. It was believed that the tears of a deceased person's friends were collected in such a bottle and placed in the grave with him. We'd find it pretty hard to collect tears in a bottle. But David is asking God to gather up His tears one by one, record them in His book, and store them up in His bottle like good wine, since those tears are precious to Him. David knew that his loving God cared deeply about the things that were troubling him and that God would do something about them.

Jesus Christ, the Son of God, came to this world to do something about our tears; to put those precious tears of ours into "His bottle," as it were, and to be with us also when we weep, because He Himself knows what it means to weep. "Blessed are those who mourn," said Jesus in the Beatitudes, "for they shall be comforted" (Mt 5:4).

All this Jesus has done for us. It took blood, sweat, and tears. You look at the agony of our Lord's Passion, and it's really very touching emotionally. It almost makes you want to cry. And you begin to wonder: "All this He has done for us. What can we do for Him? Shall we weep for Him?" That's what the weeping women did on the way to the cross. But Jesus told them, "Do not weep for Me, but weep for yourselves and your children" (Lk 23:28). Blessed are they who mourn. We think of the hymn we're going to sing at the end of this service:

> But drops of grief can ne'er repay
> The debt of love I owe;
> Here, Lord, I give myself away,
> 'Tis all that I can do. (*LSB* 437:5)

We will continue to weep from time to time as long as we live. When we fail miserably at something, we may weep. When our feelings have been hurt, we may weep. When a loved one dies, we most certainly will weep.

But Jesus is right there with us. He understands our pain. He promises us healing and comfort. On that future day in heaven, the formula ultimately will work to perfection: "His tears plus our tears equals no tears," as He promises in Revelation:

> Then I saw a new heaven and a new earth. . . . And I saw the holy city . . . and I heard a loud voice from the throne saying, "Behold, the dwelling of God is with men. . . . God Himself will be with them; He will wipe away every tear from their eyes, and death shall be no more, neither shall there be mourning nor crying nor pain any more." (Rev 21:1–4)

Hang in there with Him! His tears plus our tears equals no tears. That's a promise.

Lent 4

You've Got to Have Heart

Mark 14:34; John 16:22; Ezekiel 36:26

Tonight we delve into the very heart of our Lord and His Passion. We have completed the first triad of our journey from agony to ecstasy. Tonight we begin the second triad: heart, hands, and voices.

Yes, we're at the very heart of our Lord's Passion, and it is all centered in the cross on which He died for you and me. I think it would be appropriate and meaningful if we all stood up at this time and pledged our allegiance to that cross. Let's do it with the same motion and fervor we show when we pledge allegiance to the flag of our great nation. The words are printed in the bulletin:

> I pledge allegiance to the cross of our Lord Jesus Christ, and to the faith for which it stands; one Savior, eternal, with mercy and grace for all!

Did you notice what we did with our right hands as we made that pledge? We fervently put our hands on our hearts, of course. That's because our hearts are so vital. We can't live without them. The heart is the seat of life and strength. That's why we speak of the heart so much in our everyday lives. We say, "Have a heart" or "Stop! You're breaking my heart" or "Cross my heart and hope to die" (which isn't really a very good thing to say). We speak of heavy hearts and broken hearts, heart attacks and heart transplants, and we give out hearts on Valentine's Day. Our hearts are extremely precious to us, and we need to take care of them.

Tonight we take a careful look at the heart of Jesus—and then at our own hearts in relationship to Him.

Would you believe that the word *heart* is used almost one thousand times in the Holy Bible? In the Hebrew Old Testament, it is the word *leb* or *lebab*; in the Greek New Testament, it is *kardia*, as in our English word *cardiac*. In addition to being translated "heart," as it is most of the time, it is also translated as "mind," "spirit," and some other words. By the same token, the Greek and Hebrew words for "soul" and "spirit" are sometimes translated "heart." Thus these three important words that describe what our human life is really all about are sometimes used interchangeably, and they often refer to what we call "the seat of our emotions or our feelings."

In our first text we hear Jesus saying, "My soul [My heart] is very sorrowful [or heavy], even to death" (Mk 14:34).

37

Here we go again. Jesus is truly God. Last week we heard that He, who is God, wept. Tonight, we find Him so full of sorrow that His heart is breaking. It's almost as if He were saying, "I can't take any more of this suffering; I wish I were dead."

Does God have emotions? Does God have feelings? Of course He does. He can, for example, laugh. Ps 2:4 says, "He who sits in the heavens laughs." God can be very angry or sad. We know that He displayed anger over the people at the time of Noah, over the cities of Sodom and Gomorrah, and over the disobedience of His people before the destruction of Jerusalem. God also can be quite joyful. Scripture says that the angels rejoice, that there is joy in heaven over one sinner who repents (Lk 15:7, 10). Yes, God has emotions and feelings! After all, since the first humans were created in the image of God, their emotions reflected His. As God re-creates us and conforms us to the image of His Son, our laughter, our sense of humor, our sorrow, and our righteous anger reflect God's attitudes. Healthy emotions, properly expressed, are good and Godlike!

Right now—tonight—we hear Jesus saying, "My heart, My soul, is exceedingly sorrowful, even unto death." He begged His disciples to stay with Him in His misery while He went a stone's throw from them to pray. We learn a few things from this. For one, "misery loves company," as we say; and when we feel low, it's good to talk it over with friends and especially with our heavenly Father. That is prayer, very private prayer.

Later, on the cross, Jesus' agony of sorrow was even greater. He prayed, "My God, My God, why hast Thou forsaken Me?" (Mk 15:34). Jesus was abandoned by His Father as He suffered for our sins. As a result of His suffering on our behalf, the Father will never abandon us. He is always available to us in our darkest moments of need. Our God "never yet forsook in need The soul that trusted Him indeed" (*LSB* 750:7).

Why do you think Jesus, the Son of God, was so extremely sad? He was called upon to bear all the sorrows and sins of all people—past, present, and future. That's a mighty heavy load. Sometimes, after a busy pastoral day, ministering to many of the sorrows and problems of God's people, I come home completely drained and somewhat saddened. But that's only a tiny fraction of the sorrows and sins Jesus bore. He was bearing the sins and sorrows of the whole world at this moment—especially the sins of the heart, where most of our sins and sorrows begin. As Gen 6:5 reports, "The Lord saw that the wickedness of man was great in the earth, and that every imagination of the thoughts of his heart was only evil continually." And our Lord Jesus Christ commented, "Out of the heart come evil thoughts, murder, adultery, fornication, theft, false witness, slander" (Mt 15:19).

Look at your own heart and life for a moment. Isn't it true that those awful, mean, hurtful words you spoke to someone recently; that laziness to do your job or homework well; those words and actions of immorality and dishonesty—that all these sins are really born in the heart?

No wonder the heart of Jesus was sorrowful, even unto death. There in the Garden of Gethsemane and later on the cross He was carrying all those sins of your heart and mine, and He effectively carried them to His death in our place. That was the terrible agony that He bore for us so we might have the ecstasy of a heart that is right with God.

Look, this is how it works—and we who have been baptized into Christ's death and resurrection must remember this daily, over and over, as long as we live. He takes these sin-stained hearts of ours, He cleanses them with His own blood, and He makes them white as snow. That's why we sing and pray so frequently in our worship the words of David, "Create in me a clean heart, O God, and renew a right spirit within me" (cf. Ps 51:10). That's why the promise was made to each and every one of us in Ezekiel: "A new heart I will give you, and a new spirit I will put within you; and I will take out of your flesh the heart of stone, and give you a heart of flesh" (Ezek 36:26). That's why, when we have heavy, sorrowful hearts, He promises: "Let not your hearts be troubled; believe in God, believe also in Me. . . . I am the way, the truth, and the life" (Jn 14:1, 6). "So you have sorrow now, but I will see you again, and your hearts will rejoice" (Jn 16:22).

All this Jesus has done and continues to do for us. And what do you suppose He expects from us in return? He reminds us, "You shall love the Lord your God with all your heart, and with all your soul, and with all your mind" (Mt 22:37). And He promises us a Comforter, the Holy Spirit, to enable us to do just that. He urges us to pray:

> Ah, dearest Jesus, holy Child,
> Prepare a bed, soft, undefiled,
> A quiet chamber set apart
> For You to dwell within my heart. (*LSB* 358:13)

He wants us to have thankful hearts and lives—and we're going to sing about that at the close of this service: "Now thank we all our God With hearts and hands and voices" (*LSB* 895:1).

"My son, my daughter," says He, "give Me your heart."

I am reminded of the little boy who was celebrating Christmas. As the Scriptures were read, he saw the heavens open before those lucky shepherds who heard the angels sing and then hurried to worship. He watched the Wise Men bring gold, frankincense, and myrrh. And he thought to himself:

> What can I give Him, poor as I am?
> If I were a shepherd, I would bring a lamb;
> If I were a wise man, I would do my part;
> Yet what can I give Him: give my heart. ("In the Bleak Midwinter," stanza 4)

Lent 5

You're in Good Hands

Mark 14:41c, 46; Luke 24:39; 1 Timothy 2:8; Luke 23:46

We continue our Lenten journey through the agony and the ecstasy of our Lord's Passion and our own lives. We have considered the blood, the sweat, and the tears. We have entered the second triad: heart and hands and voices. Tonight, it's hands—all kinds of hands: your hands, my hands, Jesus' hands, the angels' hands, and our Father's hands.

Look at your hands for a moment. Go on, hold them up. Look at them carefully. Are they large or small? Are they soft or calloused? Your hands say much about you. Your hands are like the millions of snowflakes that paint a remarkable winter landscape. When you think about the amazing individuality of fingerprints and the size and shape of hands, you realize there are no hands exactly like yours. Delicate or durable, weak or strong, your hands can do all sorts of things: good or bad, creative or destructive, hurtful or helpful. Those hands of yours are precious and useful. They are a phenomenal creation of God. Perhaps that is why hands are mentioned 1,605 times in the Bible.

I want you to remember four basic things about hands. Remember them as long as you live.

1. God has "the whole world in His hands"—including your own life—and that includes the awful agony our Savior endured in His Passion.

2. Those hands of Jesus were real flesh-and-bone hands; and they really were pierced for the sins of our hands.

3. Our own hands are capable of doing either good or evil, depending on what our heart is like.

4. You're in good hands when your life is in the hands of your heavenly Father.

Let's expand those four important thoughts with more about what the Bible says about hands.

"He's Got the Whole World in His Hands"

(Sing the first stanza of "He's Got the Whole World in His Hands.") Don't ever forget these words. Our God created the whole universe, and He still runs it. History is

"*His*-story"! In Psalm 95, the psalmist says, "In His hand are the depths of the earth; the heights of the mountains are His also. The sea is His, for He made it; for His hands formed the dry land" (Ps 95:4–5).

That can be a terrible thing if we are not the children of our heavenly Father through Christ. The writer to the Hebrews said, "It is a fearful thing to fall into the hands of the living God" (10:31).

It is also a very real thing. When Jesus was on trial before Pontius Pilate, the governor said to Him, "Do You not know that I have power to release You and power to crucify You?" Jesus answered, "You would have no power over Me unless it had been given you from above" (Jn 19:10–11).

This absolute rule of God is, at the same time, wonderful for us. That awful suffering and death of Jesus in our stead was by the hand and will of God. God "did not spare His own Son but gave Him up for us all" (Rom 8:32). Isaiah said, "It was the will of the Lord to bruise Him" (Is 53:10) and "the Lord has laid on Him the iniquity of us all" (Is 53:6).

Those Hands of Jesus Were Real

Yes, our heavenly Father has "the whole world in His hands." But look also at the real flesh-and-bone hands of Jesus, our Savior. Those are the hands they cruelly nailed to the cross. Look at your own hands. They do not bear the scars of those awful nails. Jesus' hands do. When He appeared to His disciples after the resurrection, He showed them His hands and His feet and said, "See My hands and My feet, that it is I Myself; handle Me and see" (Lk 24:39). "He was wounded for our transgressions, He was bruised for our iniquities; upon Him was the chastisement that made us whole, and with His stripes we are healed" (Is 53:5).

> See, from His head, His hands, His feet
> Sorrow and love flow mingled down!
> Did e'er such love and sorrow meet
> Or thorns compose so rich a crown? (*LSB* 425:3)

Those wonderful healing, saving hands of Jesus—keep them always in mind. Those real flesh-and-bone hands were stretched out to heal us and to save us.

Our Hands Can Be Used for Evil or Good

And what about our hands? Are they evil or good? They are capable of doing both, of course.

Just before Jesus was crucified, St. Mark reports that Jesus told His disciples, "The Son of Man is betrayed into the hands of sinners" (Mk 14:41). And shortly afterward, "They laid hands on Him and seized Him" (Mk 14:46).

And these were religious people! Rotten, evil, violent hands! Are we any better? Do these hands of ours ever get us into trouble? Driving recklessly? Cheating on tests or fudging on income tax? Pushing or punching one another? Squandering money? Having idle or lazy hands? Of course we're guilty of these or comparable sins. And when our Lord stretched out His hands on the cross, He also died for the sins we do with our hands.

"Cleanse your hands, you sinners," says James, "and purify your hearts, you men of double mind" (4:8b). And the Lord laid on Him the iniquity of us all!

Now God asks us to use our hands in a profitable way. "I desire then that in every place the men should pray, lifting holy hands without anger or quarreling," Paul said in 1 Tim 2:8. Folding our hands in prayer is one of the greatest things we can do with our hands, as pictured in those beautiful praying hands of Albrecht Dürer. We pray for cleansed hands that do His will and serve Him:

> Two little eyes to look to God,
> Two little ears to hear his Word;
> Two little feet to walk his way,
> Hands to serve him every day.

It's only a little child's song, but how true it rings for us at any age!

You're in Good Hands

And when we know that "He's got the whole world in His hands" and that His hands were pierced for us and that our hands have been cleansed by Him, then we may also be sure every day that we are in good hands—not just in the hands of some insurance company, but safe and secure in the hands of our heavenly Father.

Jesus lived confidently that way, and He died that way. His last words before He expired on the cross were, "Father, into Thy hands I commit My spirit" (Lk 23:46).

There again are those great hands of our heavenly Father, in life and in death. For us who are children of God, it rings so very true. In Psalm 95, the psalmist says, "For He is our God, and we are the people of His pasture, and the sheep of His hand" (v. 7); we are the sheep who are guided and protected by His hand. In Psalm 91, our Lord promises, "He will give His angels charge of you to guard you in all your ways. On their hands they will bear you up, lest you dash your foot against a stone" (vv. 11–12). So even angels are pictured as having protective hands!

And Jesus promises in the climax of all these great passages, "My sheep hear My voice, and I know them, and they follow Me; and I give them eternal life; and they shall never perish; and no one shall snatch them out of My hand" (Jn 10:27–28).

This is our great ecstasy of life! Because of the agony of pierced hands that our Savior endured for us, we have the ecstasy of knowing that we're in good hands. In all situations we are in the hands of our heavenly Father. Say it every morning; say it every night: "Father, into Your hands I commit my spirit." Amen.

Lent 6

Voices That Will Be Heard

Psalm 19:1–4a; Luke 23:23; Mark 15:34, 37; Revelation 5:11–13

Our journey through the agony and ecstasy of our Lord's Passion is moving on to its final climax and conclusion. Next week—Holy Week—it's the agony and mystery and startling beauty of our crucified, God-forsaken God. Then, a week from Sunday, it's the ecstasy of our risen Redeemer.

In these six weeks we have struggled and agonized with our Savior through blood, sweat, and tears; we have felt the hurt of His heart and hands. Tonight, it's voices—voices that were heard and will be heard.

Always remember that all those agonies our Lord went through were real, and they were terrible. As a result, you and I, poor miserable sinners, enjoy the ecstasies of being children of our heavenly Father—forever! To that end:

He poured out His blood for *you!*

He sweated it out for *you!*

He shed real tears for *you!*

He suffered a broken heart for *you!*

His hands were pierced for *you!*

He cried out with a loud voice in darkness and anguish for *you!*

THE VOICE OF GOD WILL BE HEARD

Consider the voice of God. Let me remind you that the voice of God will be heard by you and me and by all people of all times, like it or not. I hope you never get lazy about listening for the voice of God speaking to you in His Word and in your worship. But even if you do, God will make Himself heard in other ways, as we read in Psalm 19: "The heavens are telling the glory of God; and the firmament proclaims His handiwork. Day to day pours forth speech, and night to night declares knowledge. There is no speech, nor are there words; their voice is not heard; yet their voice goes out through all the earth, and their words to the end of the world" (vv. 1–4). If you live in this world, there is some of God's unmistakable language that you simply must see and hear.

The voice of God is heard in other ways. You cannot go through life without facing terrible temptations that can lead to terrible sins. And that goes for you whether you are a child or a teenager, single or married, young or old; whether or not you have ever toyed with drugs or sex outside of marriage; whether you are honest in business or practice deception or fraud; whether you are a faithful church member or just plain turn your back on God.

Remember, in Holy Baptism, you became a child of God. He will keep looking for you when you wander away, even as He looked for Adam and Eve in the garden after they had eaten the forbidden fruit. "They heard the sound of the LORD God walking in the garden in the cool of the day and the man and his wife hid themselves. . . . But the LORD God called . . . 'Where are you?' And he said, 'I heard the sound of Thee . . . and I was afraid . . . I hid myself'" (Gen 3:8–10). Guilty, guilty, guilty. And Adam and Eve knew it. And God didn't hesitate to tell them so—and cursed the earth for their misdeed. But He also promised a Savior.

Christian, where are you? What is this that you have done? John and Jennifer, Ryan and Rachel, where are you? What is this that you have done? Our conscience, inscribed with God's Law, speaks up. The Holy Spirit, poured out on you in Baptism, reminds you of Jesus' words. The voice of God is still walking in the garden of your life, calling you. Listen for that voice. That same voice also promises you forgiveness through the blood, sweat, and tears of God's Son. God's voice boomed out at the Baptism and transfiguration of Jesus, "This is My beloved Son, with whom I am well pleased" (Mt 3:17). "Listen to Him" (Lk 9:35). God's voice will be heard.

THE VOICES OF EVIL ARE HEARD

Unfortunately, the voices of evil also are heard. Imagine, there stands the sinless Son of God before Pontius Pilate, who is supposed to pass judgment on Him. Even the tough Roman procurator says, "I find no fault in Him." He asks the mob, "What shall I do with Jesus?" You know what happened. St. Luke reports, "But they were urgent, demanding with loud cries that He should be crucified. And their voices prevailed" (Lk 23:23).

Now I'd like us to try a little experiment—and I hope you'll never forget it—to get the feeling of how fickle the people of God can be. Remember, this mob was comprised of mostly religious people, and it was the voices of the chief priests and rulers of the people that were the loudest. On Palm Sunday, just five days earlier, it's very possible that many of them were singing their hosannas to this Jesus.

In a moment I'm going to ask you to rise and put some drama and reality behind these mob scences. Put yourself into the mob. First, with open outstretched hands held hgih, let's say, "Hosanna to the Son of David!" (Mt 21:9). Then we'll change roles. It's only five days later. This time we're saying, "Crucify, crucify Him!" (Lk 23:21).

All right, let's stand and do it—and put all your feeling into it: "Hosanna to the Son of David! Blessed is He who comes in the name of the Lord! Hosanna in the highest!" Now that awful Good Friday chant: "Crucify, crucify Him!" How did that make you feel? Any similarities in your life?

All right, let's stand and do it—and put all your feeling into it: "Hosanna to the Son of David! Blessed is He who comes in the name of the Lord! Hosanna in the highest!" Now the awful Good Friday chant: "Crucify, crucify Him!" How did you feel? Any similarities in your life?

Jesus at one time made this sad commentary on human nature: "This people honors Me with their lips; but their heart is far from Me" (Mt 15:8). And James wrote that with the tongue "we bless the Lord and the Father, and with it we curse men, who are made in the likeness of God. From the same mouth come blessing and cursing. My brethren, this ought not to be so" (James 3:9–10).

Does your voice ever get you into trouble like that?

The Voice of Jesus Is Heard

Into that confusion of voices there comes the voice of Jesus—and it must be heard by all of us. St. Mark reports, "At the ninth hour Jesus cried with a loud voice, 'Eloi, Eloi, lama sabachthani?' which means, 'My God, My God, why hast Thou forsaken Me?' " (15:34). It is we who deserve to be forsaken by God when we say "Jesus Christ" in vain or "Go to hell" or wish for God to damn someone. But instead the Father forsook His own Son as He laid on Him also the sins of our voices. If we abuse or misuse our voices, the voice of Jesus prays for us, "Father, forgive them, for they know not what they do" (Lk 23:34).

How Our Voices Should Be Heard

Jesus in His Passion and death has redeemed and cleansed these God-given voices of ours to be used constructively, for our own good, for the good of others, in His service and to His glory.

There, at the foot of the cross, are representative people: Jesus' mother, Mary, using her voice to cry out, "Oh Jesus, my son and Son of God, help me; comfort me. My soul is pierced through as with a sword." Think of Simon Peter or Thomas crying out, "Lord, I believe; help Thou my unbelief." And think of the centurion who crucified Jesus, but who then used his voice to make a magnificent confession, as reported by St. Mark: "And when the centurion, who stood facing Him, saw that He thus breathed His last, he said, 'Truly, this man was the Son of God' " (15:39).

That's how our Lord wants us to use our voices: in the agony of great need, in our witness and service to others, and to the praise and glory of our great God! And all this is now possible for us. The agony of our Savior's blood, sweat, and tears has made possible the ecstasy of our hearts and hands and voices.

In Revelation (5:11–13), St. John reports:

Then I looked, and I heard around the throne . . . the voice of many angels, numbering myriads of myriads and thousands of thousands, saying with a loud voice, "Worthy is the Lamb who was slain, to receive power and wealth and wisdom and might and honor and glory and blessing!" And I heard every creature in heaven and on earth and under the earth and in the sea, and all therein saying, "To Him who sits upon the throne and to the Lamb be blessing and honor and glory and might forever and ever."

As a smashing conclusion to this sermon series and a joint expression of our faith, let's join myriads of angels and the saints in heaven by singing the last stanza of this hymn:

Lift we, then, our voices,
Swell the mighty flood;
Louder still and louder
Praise the precious blood! (*LSB* 433:6)

The Lord's Prayer & His Passion

REV. ROBERT C. SAUER

This series offers a study of the Lord's Prayer in light of our Savior's suffering and death as recorded in the four Gospels. As we blend the model prayer and the familiar scenes of the Passion, our prayer life takes on new and richer meaning.

Ash Wednesday

Our Father, Who Art in Heaven

Matthew 6:6–9

GOD IS JESUS' FATHER

Jesus speaks of, or prays to, God as His heavenly Father no less than eleven times in the Lenten narrative. He talks about "My Father's kingdom" (Mt 26:29) and about how He must "depart out of this world to the Father" (Jn 13:1). To Peter He said, "Do you think that I cannot appeal to My Father, and He will at once send Me more than twelve legions of angels?" (Mt 26:53), and "Put your sword into its sheath; shall I not drink the cup that the Father has given Me?" (Jn 18:11). Jesus prayed, "My Father, if it be possible, let this cup pass from Me" (Mt 26:39), and later, "My Father, if this cannot pass unless I drink it, Your will be done" (Mt 26:42). On the cross He prayed, "Father, forgive them, for they know not what they do" (Lk 23:34) and "Father, into Your hands I commit My spirit!" (Lk 23:46).

Only once does Jesus address the Father as "God." "My God, My God, why have You forsaken Me?" (Mt 27:46). Up to and after that dreadful moment, the peak of His suffering, there was an intimacy with and a trustful dependence on His Father to see Him through the agony He was appointed to endure.

His agony and death paid in full for all the sins of the world. The inspired writers make that clear: "The Father has sent His Son to be the Savior of the world" (1 Jn 4:14). "He is the propitiation for our sins, and not for ours only but also for the sins of the whole world" (1 Jn 2:2).

GOD IS OUR FATHER

Those who believe in Jesus as their Savior are joined to the family of God; they are called the children of God (Gal 3:26; 1 Jn 3:1).

The relationship we have with God, that of father and children, is illustrated in the story of a Roman emperor leading his army home after a victory. To keep the crowd back, Roman soldiers line the streets. When the emperor approaches the platform where the empress and her children are sitting, the youngest son jumps down and tries to run to him. But an officer grabs him by the arm. "You can't do that, boy," he shouts. "Do you realize who that man is? He's the emperor!" The boy pulls away, shouting back, "He may be your emperor, but he's my father!"

Because God is our Father, we, like Jesus, can "with confidence draw near to the throne of grace, that we may receive mercy and find grace to help in time of need" (Heb 4:16).

Ancient worship orders preface the Lord's Prayer with the phrase, "We are bold to pray" or "We dare to say," reflecting the privilege believers have to address the Creator of the universe with the intimate expression "Father."

The words "Our Father" also reflect the relationship we have with all the children of God, all other Christians. *I*, *me*, *my*, or *mine* never occur in the prayer. It's always *our*, *us*, or *we*. Jesus encourages us to pray in private at times, as He Himself did. The phrases He gave us to use in this model prayer, however, are not selfish requests but expressions of praise and petition that involve all of the heavenly Father's family.

That we acknowledge the Father as being "in heaven" is of great importance too. We recognize the existence of a world different from the present one, another world not marred by sin, death, and the devil, but one governed by His power where He allows none of these things. Both concepts are vital: His fatherhood, that speaks of His love for us, and also His power. We may love a person, but we are often powerless to correct or guide someone who is doing wrong. Unlike us, God our Father is both loving and powerful.

Pray Continually

In future meditations we will consider the content of our prayers as outlined in the petitions of the Lord's Prayer and reflected in the Lenten scenes. But today we look at the manner of our prayer life. Crucial is the "when and where" of prayer.

The prophet who held high offices in the Babylonian and Persian Empires, though he was a captive, is a classic model. It was his custom to go to the upstairs room in his home and pray three times a day. He even risked death rather than give up this practice. One could almost say that for him a life without prayer wasn't worth living.

Jesus prayed alone at regular intervals. There are seventeen references to His practice of prayer in the Gospels. "Rising very early in the morning, while it was still dark, [Jesus] departed and went out to a desolate place, and there He prayed" (Mk 1:35). Just before His suffering and death, in Gethsemane "He withdrew from [His disciples] about a stone's throw, and knelt down and prayed" (Lk 22:41). He encouraged His followers, "When you pray, go into your room and shut the door and pray to your Father who is in secret. And your Father who sees in secret will reward you" (Mt 6:6).

PRAYER CHANGES THINGS

But will it do any good? Does prayer really change things? Does prayer change God's plan of handling things? Or does prayer change us so that we accept what God has planned for us?

After the Lord decided to destroy the cities of Sodom and Gomorrah because their sins were so great, He told His chosen servant Abraham. There follows what must be the longest bargaining recorded in Scripture. "Will You indeed sweep away the righteous with the wicked?" Abraham pleads. "Suppose there are fifty righteous within the city. . . . Far be it from You to do such a thing, to put the righteous to death with the wicked, so that the righteous fare as the wicked! Far be that from You! Shall not the Judge of all the earth do what is just?" (Gen 18:23–25).

The Lord agrees to spare the city if He finds fifty righteous people. The bargaining doesn't stop there. Abraham suggests forty-five, then forty, then thirty, then twenty, then ten. The Lord agrees. But Sodom and Gomorrah, of course, are still destroyed.

To teach the effectiveness of being persistent in prayer, Jesus told His disciples a parable about a widow who came to the judge with a plea for justice (Lk 18:1–5). "For a while," said Jesus, "he refused, but afterward he said to himself, . . . 'I will give her justice, so that she will not beat me down by her continual coming' " (vv. 4–5). The parable concludes with the admonition to persist in prayer as Jesus promises so that "God [will] give justice to His elect, who cry to Him day and night" (Lk 18:7).

PRAYER COMMANDED

Perhaps the best answer to the question about "prayer changing things" is that results are not in our department; they are God's responsibility, not ours. We are simply urged to present our petitions because God commanded and invites believers in Christ Jesus to pray.

In his Large Catechism, Martin Luther makes much of prayer as being "just as strictly and seriously commanded as all other commandments: to have no other God, not to kill, not to steal, and so on" (Large Catechism III 6; *Concordia*, p. 408).

On the other hand, Luther also states that:

> We should be more encouraged and moved to pray because God has also added a promise and declared that it shall surely be done for us as we pray. He says in Psalm 50:15, "Call upon Me in the day of trouble; I will deliver you." And Christ says in the Gospel of St. Matthew, "Ask, and it will be given to you; . . . for everyone who asks receives" (7:7–8). Such promises certainly ought to encourage and kindle our hearts to pray with pleasure and delight.

Besides this, we should be moved and drawn to prayer. For in addition to this commandment and promise, God expects us and He Himself arranges the words and form of prayer for us. He places them on our lips for how and what we should pray [Psalm 51:15], so that we may see how heartily He pities us in our distress [Psalm 4:1], and we may never doubt that such prayer is pleasing to Him and shall certainly be answered. This ‹the Lord's Prayer› is a great advantage indeed over all other prayers that we might compose ourselves. For in our own prayers the conscience would ever be in doubt and say, "I have prayed, but who knows if it pleases Him or whether I have hit upon the right proportions and form?" Therefore, there is no nobler prayer to be found upon earth than the Lord's Prayer. We pray it daily [Matthew 6:11], because it has this excellent testimony, that God loves to hear it. We ought not to surrender this for all the riches of the world. (Large Catechism III 19–20, 22–23; *Concordia*, pp. 410–11)

As Jesus prayed to His Father in heaven, He encourages us to pray the same way, continuously, persistently, believing His command and promise. As we look forward to reviewing each part of the prayer Jesus gave us, we close with St. Paul's inspired assurance recorded in Philippians: "Do not be anxious about anything, but in everything by prayer and supplication with thanksgiving let your requests be made known to God. And the peace of God, which surpasses all understanding, will guard your hearts and your minds in Christ Jesus" (4:6–7).

Lent 2

Hallowed Be Thy Name

Matthew 6:9; Mark 14:30–31

GOOD GUYS DO BAD THINGS

What happens when bad guys do good things and good guys do bad things? Wasn't that the case when the high priest and the Sanhedrin placed Jesus under oath and judged Him guilty of blasphemy? After all, a person who claims to be the Son of God—under oath, no less—must be taken seriously. Was it not the duty of the Sanhedrin, the supreme Jewish court, to try cases like this?

Of course, they were the bad guys whose sole purpose was to get Jesus out of the way. I remember reading somewhere that there were forty-three violations of civil law in the apprehension, trial, and execution of Jesus Christ. The high priest,

Caiaphas, who led the attack, was a Sadducee, and so his behavior was understandable. The New Testament records that "the Sadducees say that there is no resurrection, nor angel, nor spirit" (Acts 23:8).

Surprising, however, is the behavior of the good guy, Simon Peter. He was not only part of the inner circle of disciples with James and John, but his name is listed first whenever the three are mentioned in the Gospels. His denial of Christ with an oath and his insistence that he doesn't even know Him comes as a shock. It cannot be excused by saying he was an impulsive man whose personality made him a strong leader one minute and a coward the next. What he said was a terrible sin against God. To make matters worse, Jesus had warned him, "Truly, I tell you, this very night, before the rooster crows twice, you will deny Me three times" (Mk 14:30). Even after the prediction, "[Peter] said emphatically, 'If I must die with You, I will not deny You' " (Mk 14:31).

His weakness was, in one word, pride. He was too sure of himself. The Bible warns us often about pride, the first of the "deadly sins" enumerated by the ancients. It has been said that pride elevates self to the place of God. Solomon reminds us, "Pride goes before destruction, and a haughty spirit before a fall" (Prov 16:18). Thirty-five years after his denial, the Holy Spirit moves Peter to write, "Clothe yourselves, all of you, with humility toward one another, for 'God opposes the proud but gives grace to the humble' " (1 Pet 5:5), a partial quotation from Proverbs. Peter had learned a few things!

The good news is that Peter did not die in his sin. After the third denial, "the Lord turned and looked at Peter. And Peter remembered the saying of the Lord. . . . And he went out and wept bitterly" (Lk 22:61–62). The good news is that when we stumble and fall in our weakness God does not give up on us. Peter repented and was forgiven.

TREAT GOD'S NAME IN A HOLY WAY

Both the Sanhedrin and Peter misused God's name. In the First Petition of the Lord's Prayer, Jesus invites us to approach the throne of our heavenly Father and make the request, "Hallowed be Your name" (Mt 6:9).

Luther and others are quick to point out that God's name is already holy, but we are to treat it in a holy way. The Second Commandment parallels this petition, "You shall not take the name of the LORD your God in vain" (Ex 20:7). On the positive side, we are exhorted to "call upon it in every trouble, pray, praise, and give thanks" (*Luther's Small Catechism*, p. 12). We pray, praise, and give thanks whether we are alone or gathered with others of the family of God to worship. According to Luther, "God's name is kept holy when the Word of God is taught in its truth and purity, and we, as the children of God, also lead holy lives according to it" (*Luther's Small Catechism*, p. 19).

There has been the tendency in the ongoing life of the Church to emphasize either the Word or the life to the neglect of the other. The Reformation swept away centuries of additions to the plain teachings of Holy Scripture, especially in regard to salvation by grace through faith alone. But the next generations downgraded the claim to "pure doctrine" and stressed the good life. "Deeds, not creeds" became the motto. The Bible speaks to both. "From childhood you have been acquainted with the sacred writings, which are able to make you wise for salvation through faith in Christ Jesus. All Scripture is breathed out by God and profitable for teaching, for reproof, for correction, and for training in righteousness, that the man of God may be competent, equipped for every good work" (2 Tim 3:15–17). The name of God is hallowed when His people hold to His Word and behave according to that Word.

On the negative side, the name of God "is profaned when people preach, teach, and say in God's name what is false and misleading. They use His name like an ornament and attract a market for falsehood. . . . Furthermore, men, by swearing, cursing, conjuring, and other such actions, grossly abuse the holy name as a cloak for their shame [1 Peter 2:16]. In the second place, God's name is profaned by an openly wicked life and works, when those who are called Christians and God's people are adulterers, drunkards, misers, enviers, and slanderers [1 Corinthians 5:11]" (Large Catechism III 41–43; *Concordia*, p. 413).

If Luther were living today, no doubt he also would warn against the careless misuse of God's name. The increase of profanity is alarming. If we are serious about restoring "family values" to stem the tide of violence, fornication, vulgarity, and dishonesty, we must start by teaching respect and reverence for God's name.

JESUS IS LORD

The disciples often address Jesus as "Lord." God told Moses His name was "I AM WHO I AM" (Ex 3:14). Hebrew translators regarded that name as so sacred it should not be spoken aloud. Therefore they used the consonants YHWH, which could be pronounced "Yahweh" or "Jehovah" instead. Subsequently, in the Greek translation of the Old Testament, YHWH was rendered as *kurios*, "Lord." Jesus attaches the name to Himself when He quotes Psalm 110, " 'The Lord said to My Lord, Sit at My right hand, until I put Your enemies under Your feet' " (Mt 22:44).

After our Lord's death and burial, the chief priests and Pharisees came to Pilate and asked him to make the sepulcher secure. In their stubborn unbelief, they called Jesus "that imposter" or "deceiver," one who pretends to be something he is not (Mt 27:63). How different is Paul's description of the Risen One in the second chapter of Philippians: "Therefore God has highly exalted Him and bestowed on Him the name that is above every name, so that at the name of Jesus every knee should bow, in heaven and on earth and under the earth, and every tongue confess that Jesus Christ is Lord, to the glory of God the Father" (2:9–11).

When we pray "Hallowed be Thy name," we also apply this petition to our Lord Jesus Christ. How it grates our ears and saddens our hearts when that holy name is used to emphasize a person's astonishment! We pray that those who misuse Jesus' name will learn its meaning as announced by the angel to a bewildered Joseph, "You shall call His name Jesus, for He will save His people from their sins" (Mt 1:21).

What's in a Name?

It is always interesting to learn the names given to infants when they are baptized. Years ago, babies were named after their sponsors. Before that, many were named for the saint on whose day the baby was born. Traditionally, babies also have been named for a parent or relative.

In Bible times, names were given because of their meaning. Judas, for example, means "praise of God." His life and character hardly reflected that. Jesus told His disciples, "It would have been better for that man if he had not been born" (Mt 26:24). Better known is the meaning of Peter's name, Cephas. Both *Cephas* (Aramaic) and *Peter* (Greek) mean "rock." Sometimes Peter was solid and firm, but not always. We do not necessarily become what our names mean.

Of greater importance than our name is that the name of God was spoken at our Baptism, as Jesus instructed the Church, "Go therefore and make disciples of all nations, baptizing them in the name of the Father and of the Son and of the Holy Spirit" (Mt 28:19). In that Baptism we were identified with our Lord. Paul writes, "As many of you as were baptized into Christ have put on Christ" (Gal 3:27).

The Lenten narrative mentions Nicodemus and Joseph of Arimathea, both members of the Sanhedrin, as the unlikely persons who prepared the body of Jesus for burial (Jn 19:38–40). Nicodemus, apparently, was the first person Jesus told about the need to be baptized: "Unless one is born of water and the Spirit, he cannot enter the kingdom of God" (Jn 3:5).

At one time, Baptism certificates were framed and hung on the wall in a child's bedroom as a daily reminder of being received into communion, or fellowship, with God. It also reminded a person of the obligation to live as a child of God and that his or her name was written in the Book of Life. When Jesus sent seventy-two of His followers to spread His Word and to heal the sick, they returned elated, telling Jesus, "Lord, even the demons are subject to us in Your name!" (Lk 10:17). While Jesus does not criticize them for their joy, He directs them to a greater joy, namely, "that your names are written in heaven" (Lk 10:20).

Malcolm Forbes, billionaire owner/publisher of *Forbes* magazine, was interviewed on *60 Minutes*. After a tour of his castles, yachts, and other possessions, he was asked about his extravagant lifestyle. He declared that he was determined to get everything he could and "live it up to the hilt" in this life because, he said, "I'm not sure about the next one." Jesus warned, "For what will it profit a man if he gains the whole world and forfeits his life?" (Mt 16:26). When compared to Mr. Forbes, we have few material possessions, but we know our names are written in God's Book of Life. This is not our doing, but His. Is there any better person to hallow His name?

Lent 3

Thy Kingdom Come

Matthew 6:10; 26:29

Perhaps no expression is used more frequently in prayer, preaching, and Christian literature than "the kingdom of God." But there are different kinds of kingdoms. The psalmist proclaims of God's kingdom of power, "His kingdom rules over all" (Ps 103:19); however, the Second Petition of the Lord's Prayer refers to God's rule in His kingdom of grace.

THE KINGDOM OF GOD'S GRACE

Asked "What is the kingdom of God?" Luther says: "Nothing other than what we learned in the Creed: God sent His Son, Jesus Christ, our Lord, into the world to redeem and deliver us from the devil's power [1 John 3:8]. He sent Him to bring us to Himself and to govern us as a King of righteousness, life, and salvation against sin, death, and an evil conscience" (Large Catechism III 51; *Concordia*, p. 414). Possibly Luther had Colossians 1 (vv. 13–14) in mind: "He has delivered us from the domain of darkness and transferred us to the kingdom of His beloved Son, in whom we have redemption, the forgiveness of sins."

Luther continues: "For the coming of God's kingdom to us happens in two ways: (a) here in time through the Word and faith [Matthew 13]; and (b) in eternity forever through revelation [Luke 19:11; 1 Peter 1:4–5]. Now we pray for both these things. We pray that the kingdom may come to those who are not yet in it, and, by daily growth that it may come to us who have received it, both now and hereafter in eternal life" (Large Catechism III 53; *Concordia*, p. 514). This petition has been called the mission prayer. To spread the Gospel was Jesus' constant concern. He urges us, "Pray earnestly to the Lord of the harvest to send out laborers into His harvest" (Mt 9:38).

A young German pastor, executed by the Nazis at age 39, said, "The church that does not exist for others is no church at all." That may seem a bit strong, but it is significant that two of the seven churches Jesus speaks to in the opening chapters of the Book of Revelation still thrive. The other five, each of which our Lord faults for various reasons, no longer exist. But the Church at Smyrna, which He commends because it is faithful to the Word, and the Church at Philadelphia, which apparently was concerned with mission outreach, are still there. Congregations must decide whether they want only to maintain themselves or to reach the unchurched.

THE KINGDOM OF GLORY

The Lenten reading recounts the kingdom of glory, the kingdom yet to come. At the Supper, Jesus promises the disciples, "I will not drink again of this fruit of the vine until that day when I drink it new with you in My Father's kingdom" (Mt 26:29). "I assign to you, as My Father assigned to Me, a kingdom, that you may eat and drink at My table in My kingdom and sit on thrones judging the twelve tribes of Israel" (Lk 22:29–30).

Jesus said to Pilate, "My kingdom is not of this world. If My kingdom were of this world, My servants would have been fighting, that I might not be delivered over to the Jews. But My kingdom is not from the world" (Jn 18:36). One of the two criminals who was crucified with our Lord also spoke of the kingdom: "Jesus, remember me when You come into Your kingdom." Jesus responded, "Truly, I say to you, today you will be with Me in Paradise" (Lk 23:42–43). The penitent criminal admits that he deserves punishment and rebukes the criminal who mocked the Savior. Of Jesus, he only asks to be remembered. He gets much more: "Today— with Me—in paradise." Paul would later echo this: "To Him who is able to do far more abundantly than all that we ask or think" (Eph 3:20). What an incentive to pray! But the account also suggests the questions: Will everyone go to heaven? If not, who will and who won't?

Phil Donahue once interviewed a prominent New York City minister on his show. When asked if he believed that only Christians would get to heaven, the minister answered without hesitation: "Everyone will be there. God is so great, so big, so forgiving. You'll be there too, Donahue!"

Donahue then asked his live audience if they believed they were going to heaven. Most of the audience raised a hand. He then asked if anyone believed he or she wasn't going to heaven, to which three or four hands went up in response. One of those individuals said she wasn't going to heaven because she wasn't one of 144,000 elected to be in heaven. (This is a teaching of Jehovah's Witnesses.) Donahue responded by asking why this women would want to be a member of a group that taught she didn't have a chance to get to heaven. Other audience members expressed their opinion that a nonchurchgoer could be as good as a person who goes to church and that a Christian is a person who is kind to everyone.

Not so. Jesus said of Himself, "For God so loved the world, that He gave His only Son, that whoever believes in Him should not perish but have eternal life. . . . Whoever believes in Him is not condemned, but whoever does not believe is condemned already, because he has not believed in the name of the only Son of God" (Jn 3:16, 18). When Jesus spoke of His Father's house having many rooms, He assured the disciples, especially Thomas, "I am the way, and the truth, and the life. No one comes to the Father except through Me" (Jn 14:6).

LIVING IN HOPE

Scripture is also clear about the priority we are to give the kingdom of glory while still on earth. The apostle urges us, "Set your minds on things that are above, not on things that are on earth" (Col 3:2). He even declares, "I count everything as loss because of the surpassing worth of knowing Christ Jesus my Lord. For His sake I have suffered the loss of all things and count them as rubbish, in order that I may gain Christ and be found in Him, not having a righteousness of my own that comes from the law, but that which comes through faith in Christ, the righteousness from God that depends on faith" (Phil 3:8–9). He then directs us to join with others who follow his example and reminds us that "our citizenship is in heaven" (Phil 3:20).

Peter also would have us think this way. In his first Epistle, he calls us names such as "elect," "obedient children," "newborn infants," "living stones," "a chosen race, a royal priesthood, a holy nation, a people for His own possession," but the phrase "sojourners and exiles" is used most (1 Pet 1:1–2:11).

LIVING WITHOUT ANXIETY

How does this affect our daily lives? For one thing, it delivers us from worry. In His Sermon on the Mount, Jesus admonishes, "Therefore I tell you, do not be anxious about your life, what you will eat or what you will drink, nor about your body, what you will put on" (Mt 6:25). He concludes this section with, "Your heavenly Father knows that you need them all. But seek first the kingdom of God and His righteousness, and all these things will be added to you. Therefore do not be anxious about tomorrow, for tomorrow will be anxious for itself. Sufficient for the day is its own trouble" (Mt 6:32–34). We are to "seek [which may be translated "go on seeking"] first the kingdom," namely, our goal, heaven; second, "His righteousness," the comforting knowledge that God in Christ has declared us righteous. Then He bids us unload worry about "tomorrow," as "tomorrow" is always beyond us.

For another thing, we are not to fear death as we already possess eternal life. The first Epistle of John stresses this truth, "And this is the testimony, that God gave us eternal life, and this life is in His Son. . . . I write these things to you who believe in the name of the Son of God that you may know that you have eternal life" (1 Jn 5:11, 13). Our Lord assured Martha, "Everyone who lives and believes in Me shall never die" (Jn 11:26).

Of course the eternal life we already have does not mean we presently experience the joy that is yet to come. Paul says of himself, "My desire is to depart and be with Christ, for that is far better. But to remain in the flesh is more necessary on your account" (Phil 1:23–24). The psalmist makes us eager for the time when we, too, will be with the Lord, "You make known to me the path of life; in Your presence there is fullness of joy; at Your right hand are pleasures forevermore" (Ps 16:11).

In fact, we live in a hostile and evil world. Yet we give glory to God despite our troubles and tribulations: "Blessed be the God and Father of our Lord Jesus Christ! According to His great mercy, He has caused us to be born again to a living hope through the resurrection of Jesus Christ from the dead, to an inheritance that is imperishable, undefiled, and unfading, kept in heaven for you" (1 Pet 1:3–4).

God's people have been called "the restless righteous." Often we lower our sights and pursue goals that we once thought would satisfy: "when I graduate," "when I get a good job," "when the children get married," "when I retire." But when that goal is achieved, we are not satisfied. Our Lord knows this. At the close of His High Priestly Prayer, He prays for us, "Father, I desire that they also, whom You have given Me, may be with Me where I am, to see My glory that You have given Me because You loved Me before the foundation of the world" (Jn 17:24).

And John, again, brings God's written Word to a close with the petition, "Amen. Come, Lord Jesus!" (Rev 22:20).

Lent 4

Thy Will Be Done on Earth as It Is in Heaven

Matthew 6:10; Mark 14:32–42

Our Lord's prayers in the Garden of Gethsemane are a most puzzling event in the account of His suffering and death. *(Read Mark 14:32–42.)*

Not only is this episode puzzling, it leads to the most difficult petition in the Lord's Prayer, "Thy will be done on earth as it is in heaven." A world of difference exists between this prayer and the Savior's High Priestly Prayer spoken immediately before the garden prayer. In the High Priestly Prayer, Jesus asks the Father to give Him the glory He had before the world began. Then He prays for His disciples, including that they be protected from the evil one. Finally, He asks the Father that all believers see His glory from before creation (Jn 17:5, 15, 24).

In the garden, Jesus prays that the cup of suffering be taken from Him. But He adds, "Yet not what I will, but what You will" (Mk 14:36).

WE, TOO, CARRY A CROSS

While we cannot comprehend the intensity of Jesus' agony, we can relate to it. We also dread the future—unpaid bills, a loved one's death, illness, disability, operations, loss of employment, long-standing family quarrels, to name a few. Or our fears, our crosses, may be those we carry because we are His disciples. Our Lord said, "If anyone would come after Me, let him deny himself and take up his cross and follow Me" (Mt 16:24).

Not every burden in life is necessarily a cross. Only those that we willingly bear because of our identification with Christ are called crosses. A broken leg, a house destroyed by fire, or a car accident are not crosses in Jesus' use of the word. However, an assistant who rejects the advances of her boss and therefore is demoted or fired truly bears a cross. A salesman who will not cheat and subsequently is assigned a poorer or smaller territory because impressive profits require dishonesty—this man carries a cross.

Or the cross may be some impediment to who we are and what we do. We believe we could be more effective if the handicap were removed. Paul asked the Lord three times to take away "a thorn . . . given me in the flesh, a messenger of Satan to harass me" (2 Cor 12:7). Paul reports the Lord's answer, "But He said to

SERMONS FOR LENT AND EASTER

me, 'My grace is sufficient for you, for My power is made perfect in weakness'"
(2 Cor 12:9).

Certainly, however, even these crosses are light when compared to the cross
upon which our Lord suffered and died. He paid the penalty for our sins, suffering
hell in our place. Now we can have forgiveness, peace, and eternal life.

God's Will Is Done

We cannot fathom what Jesus endured in the Garden of Gethsemane as He knelt,
and even prostrated Himself, on the ground. As true man, the sweat from His
agony mingled with drops of blood (Lk 22:44). Medically, we are told it is possible
for small blood vessels to break, permitting blood to mix with sweat. Jesus' bloody
sweat was so copious it formed drops that fell to the ground. He struggled alone,
the three disciples who came with Him of no help at all. Isaiah's prophecy is fulfilled: "I have trodden the winepress alone" (63:3). And Jesus' loneliness was just
beginning—soon each of the Twelve would forsake Him.

Was Jesus' prayer ignored? Is prayer ever? Far from it. The cup stays, the
Father's will prevails, but "there appeared to Him an angel from heaven, strengthening Him" (Lk 22:43). With renewed energy Jesus doesn't wait for Judas and the
crowd to arrive, but takes the initiative as He rouses the disciples: "Rise, let us be
going; see, My betrayer is at hand" (Mk 14:42).

Who Can Understand?

One thousand years ago, the first of six forceful and futile attempts to establish
Christian rule in the Holy Land took place. Great spiritual rewards were promised
to those who participated. Thousands from all over Europe lost their lives in what
history calls the Crusades. The motto "God wills it" was the battle cry. But was this
God's will? Does God will everything that happens?

It is not possible to comprehend God. As someone observed, "If I could understand God, I would be God." We do not hesitate to join in Paul's doxology: "Oh, the
depth of the riches and wisdom and knowledge of God! How unsearchable are His
judgments and how inscrutable His ways! 'For who has known the mind of the
Lord, or who has been His counselor?'" (Rom 11:33–34). Toward the end of his
miseries, Job admits, "I have uttered what I did not understand, things too wonderful for me, which I did not know" (42:3).

Even so, by the grace of God and with the guidance of the Holy Spirit as we
hold firmly to God's Word, we can arrive at certain conclusions. God has a single
will, but because of our limited comprehension, He lets us see Himself with both a
revealed will and a hidden will. In His Word, God reveals that He wants sinners

saved. Jesus said, "For this is the will of My Father, that everyone who looks on the Son and believes in Him should have eternal life" (Jn 6:40).

It is also God's revealed will that believers lead godly lives. Inspired by the Holy Spirit, Paul writes, "This is the will of God, your sanctification" (1 Thess 4:3). But there are certain spiritual truths that God keeps hidden; the Bible does not furnish us with answers to every question we ask. "No one comprehends the thoughts of God except the Spirit of God" (1 Cor 2:11).

God's Word also demonstrates an irresistible and a resistible will of God. No one has a choice about being present on Judgment Day: "For we will all stand before the judgment seat of God" (Rom 14:10). Jesus stresses this in the parables of the wheat and weeds (Mt 13:24–30, 36–43), the good and bad fish (Mt 13:47–50), and the sheep and goats (Mt 25:31–46). However, God's will can be resisted regarding salvation. God "desires all people to be saved and to come to the knowledge of the truth" (1 Tim 2:4). He "is patient toward you, not wishing that any should perish, but that all should reach repentance" (2 Pet 3:9). However, many will reject the Word and "resist the Holy Spirit," as Stephen said the Jewish leaders did (Acts 7:51).

God also reveals that what He permits may differ from what He ordains. God does not want us to sin, but He allows it to happen. Certain things are ordained: "He has fixed a day on which He will judge the world in righteousness by a man whom He has appointed" (Acts 17:31).

The Devil, the World, and Our Sinful Selves

In the Small Catechism, Luther identifies three sources that oppose God's good and gracious will: the devil, the world, and our sinful nature. We see them at work in the account of Jesus' Passion. It begins by noting that the devil "entered into Judas called Iscariot, who was of the number of the twelve. He went away and conferred with the chief priests and officers how he might betray Him to them" (Lk 22:3–4). This was not the usual demonic possession that our Lord encountered throughout His ministry. Here the mind, heart, and will of the betrayer were taken over by the evil one.

Simon Peter's vehement denial of Jesus, swearing "I do not know the man" (Mt 26:72, 74), is a prime example of the world opposing God's will. So are Pontius Pilate, with his contempt for truth; the mob that cried, "Let Him be crucified!" (Mt 27:22); and those who insulted and mocked Jesus, saying, "You who would destroy the temple and rebuild it in three days, save Yourself!" (Mt 27:40).

Humanity's "sinful nature," in opposition to God's will, surfaces when the Twelve abandon Jesus in Gethsemane shortly after Jesus admonishes Peter: "The spirit indeed is willing, but the flesh is weak" (Mt 26:41).

There is another meaning to the word *will*. It is a document that identifies who shall receive our possessions when we die. Normally, parents name each other or children as beneficiaries. On the cross, Jesus, a loving son, provides a will for His mother. "When Jesus saw His mother and the disciple whom He loved standing nearby, He said to His mother, 'Woman, behold, your son!' Then He said to the disciple, 'Behold, your mother!' And from that hour the disciple took her to his own home" (Jn 19:26–27).

That same loving Son names us heirs to an eternal future in a home where the will of God is done without opposition. "Let not your hearts be troubled. Believe in God; believe also in Me. In My Father's house are many rooms. If it were not so, would I have told you that I go to prepare a place for you? And if I go and prepare a place for you, I will come again and will take you to Myself, that where I am you may be also" (Jn 14:1–3).

Lent 5

Give Us This Day Our Daily Bread

Matthew 6:11; John 19:23–24

The first three petitions deal with lofty spiritual matters: the holy name of God, His kingdom, and His will. Rather abruptly, Jesus next directs us to ask the Father for an apparently less important request, "Give us this day our daily bread" (Mt 6:11). But Christianity also shows concern for material things, otherwise why would our Lord turn water into wine, heal the sick, feed the five thousand, give sight to the blind, speech to the dumb, and hearing to the deaf? Possibly, Christianity is the most material of all religions. With the spread of faith, hospitals are built to care for the ill, orphans are housed, and food and clothing are distributed to the poor.

A BROAD "BREAD"

However, we need not limit "bread" to mean only the food bakers prepare. We would agree with Luther that it includes "everything that has to do with the support and needs of the body" (*Luther's Small Catechism*, p. 21). We would also support Catechism explanations that the words "this day" and "daily" intend to teach us to live contentedly.

Throughout the Lenten account, the lack of contentment with their daily bread is evident both on the part of the disciples and those who plotted against Christ. Neither the Twelve nor the chief priests and elders were content with their station in life. Shortly after the Lord's Supper was instituted, "a dispute also arose among [the disciples], as to which of them was to be regarded as the greatest" (Lk 22:24). Even the Jewish leaders, who already held high offices, could not tolerate the thought that someone else was more important than they: "Look, the world has gone after Him" (Jn 12:19). Pilate recognizes their jealousy: "For he knew that it was out of envy that they had delivered Him up" (Mt 27:18).

It has been said that envy "does not want more for self, but less for others." The trail of envy can be traced throughout Scripture. Cain envies his brother Abel and becomes the first murderer. Joseph's brothers will not put up with his dreams of ruling over them, so they sell him as a slave and lie about his disappearance. In his brief letter to Gaius, St. John writes, "Diotrephes, who likes to put himself first, does not acknowledge our authority. So if I come, I will bring up what he is doing, talking wicked nonsense against us. And not content with that, he refuses to welcome the brothers, and also stops those who want to and puts them out of the church" (3 Jn 9–10). Envy, then, is a bridge that leads to evil.

CONTENT WITH POSSESSIONS

While some are unhappy with their situation in life, others are not content with their possessions. Our Lord's warning is simple and profound: "Be on your guard against all covetousness, for one's life does not consist in the abundance of his possessions" (Lk 12:15). There are many kinds of greed. The Passion history spotlights Judas's love of money but also mentions the soldiers beneath the cross gambling for the seamless garment Jesus wore. Jews wore five articles of clothing: sandals, turban, girdle, inner garment, and outer cloak. The four soldiers divided four of these among themselves but "cast lots" for the more expensive item (Jn 19:23–24). This custom of the soldiers "inheriting" a crucified man's clothing was the final indignity for a dying criminal.

The soldiers' game was different from gambling today. They did not bet their own money with the hope of winning a greater sum. Nor was their livelihood threatened if they lost. Only two states do not allow gambling of any kind, but in the other 48 states, gambling revenue rose 7 percent in 2006 to more than $32 billion.[4] The temptation to gamble becomes greater when milder terms replace offensive ones—"gambling" is called "gaming"; "wager" replaces "bet." And when states "legalize" various practices, it tends to make them appear morally acceptable.

---

4 www.americangaming.org/Press/press_releases/press_detail.cfv?ID=432

Our denomination, through its Commission on Theology and Church Relations, issued a report on gambling for study and discussion. According to the report, gambling "encourages the sins of greed and covetousness," "promotes the mismanagement of possessions entrusted to us by God," "works at cross purposes with a commitment to productive work," "is a potentially addictive behavior," and "threatens the welfare of our neighbor and militates against the common good." The report also says that "some Christians have taken the position that certain behaviors (such as any form of dancing, smoking, alcoholic consumption, the cinema, card games, certain forms of music, and the like) are sinful *because they can (and often do)* lead to sinful behavior." Caution is called for as we must "refrain from declaring each and every act [as] in and of itself contrary to the Word of God and therefore sinful."[5]

The other extreme is echoed in expressions such as "Life is a gamble"; or "Every time you drive your car on a highway, you're gambling with your life and the lives of others"; or "Isn't investing in a business or playing the stock market gambling? You can lose everything you put into it."

One of the best commentaries on the dangers of desiring material wealth is Paul's to Timothy: "Now there is great gain in godliness with contentment, for we brought nothing into the world, and we cannot take anything out of the world. But if we have food and clothing, with these we will be content. But those who desire to be rich fall into temptation, into a snare, into many senseless and harmful desires that plunge people into ruin and destruction. For the love of money is a root of all kinds of evils. It is through this craving that some have wandered away from the faith and pierced themselves with many pangs" (1 Tim 6:6–10). The love of money, not money itself, is "a root of all kinds of evils" (v. 10). It is not wrong to be rich. A few sentences after the "love of money" warning, the apostle asks Timothy to counsel those who are rich to put their hope in God and be generous in sharing their wealth (1 Tim 6:17–19). Even so, our Lord warns, "Only with difficulty will a rich person enter the kingdom of heaven. Again I tell you, it is easier for a camel to go through the eye of a needle than for a rich person to enter the kingdom of God" (Mt 19:23–24).

BE CONTENT WITH OTHER PEOPLE

In addition to being content with our station in life and our possessions, we are also admonished to be content with the gift of friends and others who are close to us. In his Small Catechism definition of daily bread, Luther includes "a devout husband or wife, devout children, devout workers, devout and faithful rulers, . . .

---

5 Commission on Theology and Church Relations, LCMS, *Gambling* (St. Louis: The Lutheran Church—Missouri Synod, 1996), 6–14 (*original emphasis*).

good friends, faithful neighbors" (*Luther's Small Catechism*, p. 21). One is hard pressed to read about any of these in the Lenten account, but there are some. Not counting the disciples, whose friendship and loyalty wavered between hot and cold, there is the owner of the house who furnished the Upper Room for the Passover feast; another unnamed person who responded to Jesus' cries on the cross by offering Him a sponge with wine vinegar for Him to drink (Mt 27:48); and Joseph of Arimathea, "a disciple of Jesus, but secretly for fear of the Jews, [who] asked Pilate that he might take away the body of Jesus, and Pilate gave him permission. So he came and took away His body. Nicodemus also, who earlier had come to Jesus by night, came" (Jn 19:38–39). They buried Jesus in a new tomb that belonged to Joseph (Jn 19:40–41).

Perhaps the most loyal of our Lord's friends were the women and the others who followed Him to Calvary, mourning and wailing. Jesus told them, "Daughters of Jerusalem, do not weep for Me, but weep for yourselves and for your children. For behold, the days are coming when they will say, 'Blessed are the barren and the wombs that never bore and the breasts that never nursed!'" (Lk 23:28–29). In particular, His mother's sister, Mary the wife of Clopas, and Mary of Magdala stood with His mother near the cross (Jn 19:25). As a reward for their faithfulness, several of them would be the first to hear of and announce the good news of Jesus' resurrection.

Involved in the Answer

As in the petition regarding forgiveness, we are involved in the answer to this petition. Many people, including children, go to bed hungry each night, even in our affluent country, though there is enough food for all. The supply is there; the distribution is wanting. St. John reminds us, "If anyone has the world's goods and sees his brother in need, yet closes his heart against him, how does God's love abide in him? Little children, let us not love in word or talk but in deed and in truth" (1 Jn 3:17–18).

Should this be difficult for us? Not at all, especially when we consider how much the heavenly Father gives to us. The word *give* occurs more than two thousand times in the Bible. Jesus mentions the Father's giving fourteen times in His High Priestly Prayer (John 17). The concept is no less real in Luther's Small Catechism: "He has given me my body and soul, eyes, ears, and all my members. . . . He will . . . give eternal life to me and all believers in Christ. . . . God certainly gives daily bread to everyone. . . . [He] gives eternal salvation to all who believe this. . . . In the Sacrament, forgiveness of sins, life, and salvation are given us through these words" (*Luther's Small Catechism*, pp. 15, 17, 20, 24, 31). All these gifts come with or are a result of God's gift to us, Jesus Christ, who "who gave Himself for us to redeem us from all lawlessness and to purify for Himself a people for His own possession who are zealous for good works" (Titus 2:14).

Lent 6

Forgive Us Our Trespasses as We Forgive Those Who Trespass against Us

Matthew 6:12; Luke 23:34

"I'll sue!" Whatever a person's reason for taking this action against his neighbor—greed, pride, anger, the desire to get even—there is a world of difference between it and the Savior's first words from the cross, "Father, forgive them, for they know not what they do" (Lk 23:34). It also runs counter to the Fifth Petition of the Lord's Prayer, "Forgive us our trespasses as we forgive those who trespass against us." (Modern translations use "debts" and "debtors" for "trespasses" in Matthew's account. Luke uses "sins" and "indebted.")

THE FORGIVEN FORGIVE

Like so many frequently used words, *forgive* has lost its full meaning. The psalmist observes, "As far as the east is from the west, so far does He *remove* our transgressions from us" (Ps 103:12, *emphasis added*). Speaking through the prophet Isaiah, the Lord comforts His wayward people Israel, "I, I am He who *blots out* your transgressions for My own sake, and I will *not remember* your sins" (Is 43:25, *emphasis added*).

Jesus' message of forgiveness was a vital part of His ministry. Before He healed the paralytic, He met the man's greater need, "My son, your sins are forgiven" (Mk 2:5). This angered the religious leaders more than the healing.

Even the disciples had to learn, as we do, that forgiveness is not a one-time action: "Peter came up and said to Him, 'Lord, how often will my brother sin against me, and I forgive him? As many as seven times?' Jesus said to him, 'I do not say to you seven times, but seventy times seven'" (Mt 18:21–22). Nor is forgiveness followed by refusing to interact with the offender in the future. After forgiveness, says Luther, we will "gladly do good to those who sin against us" (*Luther's Small Catechism*, p. 21).

This is a large order—but not if we keep in mind that the essence of God is love (1 Jn 4:8) and the center of His love is forgiveness made possible by the death and resurrection of Jesus Christ.

Our Lord's emphasis on forgiveness did not end with His words on the cross. He taught us how to deal with the vexing problem of people hurting people, of returning evil for evil. "Christ also suffered for you," writes Peter, "leaving you an example, so that you might follow in His steps. He committed no sin, neither was deceit found in His mouth. When He was reviled, He did not revile in return; when He suffered, He did not threaten" (1 Pet 2:21–23). Christ left us a model of behavior when we are wronged. Stephen, the first martyr, became a prime example. His last words were, "Lord, do not hold this sin against them" (Acts 7:60).

REPENTANCE AND FORGIVENESS

Jesus adds a reason to His plea for forgiveness: "They know not what they do." Does ignorance excuse wrongdoing?

Ignorance does not remove guilt, much less pay for wrongdoing. Repentance is the solution, followed by assurance of forgiveness. Strangely enough, Judas is the only person in the Passion narrative who admits, "I have sinned" (Mt 27:4). His confession is brushed aside by the chief priests and elders: "What is that to us? See to it yourself" (Mt 27:4). He then tries to transfer the guilt to the thirty pieces of silver by throwing them into the temple. It doesn't work. Guilt-ridden, Judas suicides.

Peter accuses the crowd and they cry: "Brothers, what shall we do?" (Acts 2:37). Peter replies, "Repent and be baptized every one of you in the name of Jesus Christ for the forgiveness of your sins. . . . So those who received his word were baptized" (Acts 2:38, 41).

Again, we ponder Jesus' words, "They know not what they do." Who are "they"? The next sentence describes the soldiers dividing the Savior's clothing, so we might assume He was referring to them, but they were simply carrying out orders when they nailed Him to a cross. After the resurrection, Peter heals a crippled man, then addresses the men of Israel: "You killed the Author of life. . . . Now, brothers, I know that you acted in ignorance, as did also your rulers" (Acts 3:15, 17). Still later, Paul mentions that "those who live in Jerusalem and their rulers . . . did not recognize [Jesus]" (Acts 13:27). The accusations made by Peter and Paul identify "they" as the rulers and the people of Jerusalem. We are aware of a state of mind called "mob mentality." For fear of ridicule, otherwise fair-minded people may follow the crowd though they do not agree with what is happening.

In its deepest meaning, the entire human race is responsible for our Lord's suffering and death.

In the Lord's Prayer, we promise God that because we are forgiven, we will forgive anyone who sins against us as did the father of the prodigal son. His son sinned against him by misusing his inheritance, deserting the family, and living a profligate life. But the father welcomes him back and does not demand anything. He just forgives and starts life anew, in joy.

Maundy Thursday

Lead Us Not into Temptation

Matthew 6:13; John 11:47–50

Because any temptation to sin is such a threat to our faith, we do well to understand the phrase "Lead us not into temptation" (Mt 6:13). The English equivalent falls short of the biblical term. "Keep us from situations in which we could fall into temptation" is most likely what is meant. Some newer Bible translations render it, "Do not put us to the test" (New Jerusalem Bible).

GOD DOES TEST US

But God does test us, and for good reason. He allowed Satan to test the faith of Job, first by destroying his livestock and then even his sons and daughters. In the end, Job survives, keeps his faith, and is doubly blessed.

From time to time, Jesus would test His followers' faith. When He was preaching to a large crowd, He asked His disciple Philip, " 'Where are we to buy bread, so that these people may eat?' He said this to test him, for He Himself knew what He would do" (Jn 6:5–6). Another test occurs when a Canaanite woman pleads with Jesus to help her demon-possessed daughter (Mt 15:21–28). First, He ignores her. Finally, He advises her that He was sent only to the lost sheep of Israel. She persists, but He replies, "It is not right to take the children's bread and throw it to the dogs" (v. 26). "Yes, Lord," she says, "yet even the dogs eat the crumbs that fall from their masters' table" (v. 27). He applauds her faith and grants her request. Such testing brings us closer to the Lord.

SATAN TESTS TO SIN

Temptations to sin, however, come from the devil who works through the world and our sinful nature. In his first Epistle, John warns: "For all that is in the world—

the desires of the flesh and the desires of the eyes and pride in possessions—is not from the Father but is from the world" (1 Jn 2:16). The term *world* is everything that has become evil in God's creation. So John adds, "The whole world lies in the power of the evil one" (1 Jn 5:19).

There are many different temptations. Like weeds that grow in all sorts of soil, so temptations abound in virtually any situation. Because of our sinful nature, each of us has certain weaknesses that others may not have. We are vulnerable when we think we will not fall into temptations that, for the moment, do not appeal to us: "I would never do that!" Undoubtedly, this is what Paul had in mind when he warned the Corinthians: "Let anyone who thinks that he stands take heed lest he fall" (1 Cor 10:12).

The Passion account includes a temptation that is attractive but deceptive because it appears to have a proper goal. Upset with the growing popularity of Jesus, members of the Sanhedrin complained, "If we let Him go on like this, everyone will believe in Him, and the Romans will come and take away both our place and our nation" (Jn 11:48). But Caiaphas had the answer: "It is better for you that one man should die for the people, not that the whole nation should perish" (v. 50). He was raging, "We must kill Him for the good of the nation." This sounds like the expressions "The end justifies the means" and "It's not quite right, but it's for a good cause."

THERE IS HELP!

Each temptation appears to offer pleasure. To deal with them, our Lord first wants us to be aware of who employs such deceptions—the devil, our archenemy. Jesus calls him "a liar and the father of lies" (Jn 8:44).

Second, when temptation comes, we must take a stand against it. A wavering decision is like sliding down an icy hill and hoping we'll stop before hitting bottom. Jesus told the sleeping disciples, "Watch and pray that you may not enter into temptation" (Mt 26:41).

Third, we are not alone in the battle. Jesus assured an overconfident Peter, "Simon, Simon, behold, Satan demanded to have you, that he might sift you like wheat, but I have prayed for you that your faith may not fail" (Lk 22:31–32). But didn't Peter lose faith? He did not lose saving faith—belief that Jesus was his Savior and Lord. He did, however, lose trust in God as his defender and protector. He also lost faith in his own strength. This same Jesus who prayed for him "is at the right hand of God, [and] indeed is interceding for us" (Rom 8:34).

Another help in our struggle with temptation is the Sacrament Jesus instituted on the night He was betrayed. With the bread He gives us His body, and with the cup of wine, His blood. In his Large Catechism, Luther writes, "There are so many hindrances and temptations of the devil and of the world that we often become weary and faint, and sometimes we also stumble [Hebrews 12:3]. Therefore, the Sacrament is given as a daily pasture and sustenance, that faith may refresh and strengthen itself [Psalm 23:1–3] so that it will not fall back in such a battle, but become ever stronger and stronger" (Large Catechism V 23–24; *Concordia*, p. 434).

In addition to prayer and the Supper, there is the Word of God itself. The first Sunday in Lent we hear how the devil tempted Jesus after His forty-day fast in the desert. Each of the three temptations is a shortcut to a desired goal; each suggests flattery; each speaks to a basic need in life. Jesus answers each suggestion with Scripture, and the devil leaves Him (Mt 4:1–11). We, too, can call on the powerful Word of God: "Put on the whole armor of God, that you may be able to stand against the schemes of the devil. . . . Take the helmet of salvation, and the sword of the Spirit, which is the Word of God" (Eph 6:11, 17).

Good Friday

Deliver Us from Evil

Matthew 6:13

When a child reaches a certain age, almost any order is answered with the question, "Why?"

"Come in out of the rain, or you'll get wet." "Why?"

"It's getting dark; time to go to bed." "Why?"

No answer satisfies!

THE "WHY" QUESTION

Three "why" questions appear in the Passion of our Lord—none of which is answered. Jesus asks Judas "why": "Friend, why have you come?" (Mt 26:50 NKJV). The second question is Pilate's to the leaders of the people: "Why, what evil has He done?" (Lk 23:22). Jesus asks the third question as He hangs on the cross: "My God, My God, why have You forsaken Me?" (Mt 27:46). Can this be? God forsaken by God? It is impossible to penetrate the divine mystery and workings of the Holy Trinity. Earlier in His ministry, our Lord said of the Father, "He who sent Me is with Me. He has not left Me alone" (Jn 8:29). Could Jesus make that claim now?

Peter must have felt very alone when he denied our Lord three times. Who has not known loneliness when caught sinning? But the greatest loneliness of all was when the Father made His Son "to be sin who knew no sin, so that in Him we might become the righteousness of God" (2 Cor 5:21).

GOD USES EVIL

We are instructed to pray, "Deliver us from evil" (Mt 6:13). The greatest evil is eternal separation from God brought by unbelief. The Savior told Nicodemus, "Whoever believes in Him is not condemned, but whoever does not believe is condemned already, because he has not believed in the name of the only Son of God" (Jn 3:18).

Two thoughts compose the petition "Deliver us from evil." We must be able to recognize evil, and we must want to be delivered from evil. The handsome young Joseph illustrates both. A slave in the house of the Egyptian official Potiphar, Joseph is invited to commit adultery by Potiphar's wife. He refuses, as it would be a sin against his master, and as he puts it, "How then can I do this great wickedness and sin against God?" (Gen 39:9).

Certainly lust is a problem for many. The first sexual sins described in Scripture are the homosexual acts committed in the city of Sodom. For its wickedness, the Lord destroys Sodom and its environs with a rain of burning sulfur. We each have different weaknesses, many of which surface in the Lenten narrative—pride, envy, greed, to name a few. Christians are not exempt from sins of the heart and of the flesh.

When we experience difficulties, we may wonder if God has heard our pleas to "deliver us from evil." The writer to the Hebrews directs: "It is for discipline that you have to endure. God is treating you as sons. For what son is there whom his father does not discipline? . . . For the moment all discipline seems painful rather than pleasant, but later it yields the peaceful fruit of righteousness to those who have been trained by it" (Heb 12:7, 11).

THE FINAL DELIVERANCE

Luther closes his explanation of this last petition of the Lord's Prayer with the hope that when our last hour comes, our Father would "give us a blessed end, and graciously take us from this valley of sorrow to Himself in heaven" (*Luther's Small Catechism*, p. 22).

The Bible often pictures eternal life with our Lord in negative terms: no hunger, no thirst, no death, no mourning, no crying, no pain (Rev 7:16–17; 21:4; 22:5). When our forefathers came to North America, they were separated from loved ones for the rest of their lives. With ease of travel and communications today, the problem is not so large, but there are still heartrending separations, and death is one of these. We can make new friends, but those who have left this earth are never replaced. This touches on the age-old question, "Will we know each other in heaven?" The Holy Spirit doesn't tell us. But if you insist, how else can we explain that, at the transfiguration of our Lord, Peter recognized Moses and Elijah, who appeared with Jesus though they had died centuries ago?

If we press for more details, we need to remember that anything we understand now would be too "little" to fit the heavenly scene. Also, what pleases us now may not in the next world—even as a young girl cannot conceive of what will fulfill her desires as a woman. At the end of his chapter on love, Paul expresses it this way: "When I was a child, I spoke like a child, I thought like a child, I reasoned like a child. When I became a man, I gave up childish ways. For now we see in a mirror dimly, but then face to face. Now I know in part; then I shall know fully, even as I have been fully known" (1 Cor 13.11–12).

Isn't it enough to trust our Lord? He plainly says, "In My Father's house are many rooms. If it were not so, would I have told you that I go to prepare a place for you? And if I go and prepare a place for you, I will come again and will take you to Myself, that where I am you may be also" (Jn 14:2–3). If a good friend invites us to his home, which we have never seen, we wouldn't demand information about the room we would use, what the menu would be, or who else was invited. We would show confidence in our host by accepting the invitation with thanks. Not only that, we would anticipate with joy whatever he prepared for us.

On this note, we complete our meditations on the petitions of the Lord's Prayer as reflected in Gospel accounts of our Lord's suffering and death. There remains the triumphant doxology, "For Thine is the kingdom and the power and the glory forever and ever"—our Easter theme.

Easter Day

Thine Is the Kingdom and the Power and the Glory Forever and Ever

Matthew 6:13; 28:1–10

The irony of Easter is that the chief priests accepted the soldiers' report of Jesus' resurrection, but the disciples did not. The chief priests, who repeatedly rejected the claims of Jesus, "gave a sufficient sum of money to the soldiers and said, 'Tell people, "His disciples came by night and stole Him away while we were asleep" ' " (Mt 28:12–13). On the other hand, Luke records that "these words seemed to [the disciples] an idle tale, and they did not believe them" (Lk 24:11). If the accounts of the resurrection were fabricated, as many claim to this day, the disciples would have believed and the high priests would not. Today we proclaim hymns of praise as we joyfully confess our own God-given faith in the risen Savior.

THINE IS THE KINGDOM

The close of the Lord's Prayer, "Thine is the kingdom and the power and the glory forever and ever," while not recorded in the early Gospel accounts, reflects one of the doxologies from the Book of Revelation: "To Him who sits on the throne and to the Lamb be blessing and honor and glory and might forever and ever!" (Rev 5:13).

In equally majestic phrases, Paul describes Christ's role after His ascension: "[God] seated Him at His right hand in the heavenly places, far above all rule and authority and power and dominion, and above every name that is named, not only in this age but also in the one to come. And He put all things under His feet and gave Him as head over all things to the church, which is His body, the fullness of Him who fills all in all" (Eph 1:20–23).

Time does not permit dwelling on each detail of this grand summary, but we can detail a few. "All things under His feet" (v. 22) includes the seen and unseen parts of creation. Astronomers continue to discover that the world of planets, stars, nebulae, and whatever else is out there is far more extensive than previous generations thought. There doesn't seem to be an end to it; year after year, objects farther from Earth are discovered. "Heavenly places" (v. 20) also identifies paradise and even hell itself. There is no place where a kingdom other than Christ's exists.

All of this is comforting to us, because Paul says that the Savior is "head over all things to the church" (v. 22). In other words, He governs the world for the well-being of the Church, protecting all believers as He sees fit. Meanwhile, He Himself prays for us before the Father: "If anyone does sin, we have an advocate with the Father, Jesus Christ the righteous" (1 Jn 2:1).

THINE IS THE POWER

On Easter morning, the silence of Holy Saturday gives way to a flurry of activities as the sun rises and as God's power effects the miracle of the resurrection of a dead body. With few exceptions the power of God is dormant during the capture, trials, and execution of Jesus Christ. Only in Gethsemane are there indications of where the real power lies. Jesus asked those who want to apprehend Him: " 'Whom do you seek?' They answered Him, 'Jesus of Nazareth.' Jesus said to them, 'I am He.' . . . When Jesus said to them, 'I am He,' they drew back and fell to the ground" (Jn 18:4–6). When Peter cut off the right ear of the high priest's servant, our Lord healed him (Lk 22:50–51). Even that show of mercy and power goes unheeded. Jesus rebuked His disciple: "Do you think that I cannot appeal to My Father, and He will at once send Me more than twelve legions of angels?" (Mt 26:53).

However, the full power of Christ shines forth on Easter morning. An angel with the appearance of lightning rolled away the stone. "For fear of him the guards trembled and became like dead men" (Mt 28:4). Matthew and Mark tell of an angel who spoke to the women when they came to the tomb, and Luke and John report two angels. However, Matthew and Mark do not say that only one angel was there. After church, if you ask someone who was there, the person will name a few friends known to both of you, but that doesn't mean those persons were the only ones attending.

Over the years, various critics of the Easter account cite the discrepancies in the re-telling of the events of that morning in the four Gospels. According to Matthew, Jesus appeared first to Mary Magdalene and other women but Luke names Peter as first to see Jesus. None of the four evangelists states that the women were the first, though the context may imply it. Moreover, Luke simply mentions that "the Lord has risen indeed, and has appeared to Simon!" quoting the two disciples who met Jesus on the road to Emmaus (Lk 24:34). Nothing is said about when Peter saw Him. Critics also highlight that Luke writes about Jesus appearing to the apostles in the Jerusalem area, while Matthew says that He appeared in Galilee. Nothing in either text indicates that only one meeting took place. Luke refers to Jesus' appearance most likely in the evening on the first day of the week (Lk 24:33–36). Matthew describes a later episode at a mountain in Galilee where Jesus challenges them with the Great Commission (Mt 28:16).

THINE IS THE GLORY

The importance of the resurrection cannot be overestimated. All Christianity rests on this foundation. Paul does not exaggerate: "If Christ has not been raised, your faith is futile and you are still in your sins. Then those also who have fallen asleep in Christ have perished. If in this life only we have hoped in Christ, we are of all people most to be pitied" (1 Cor 15:17–19). It is necessary that we carefully examine the evidence regarding the absence of Jesus' body from the tomb.

Both friends and foes agree that Christ predicted His own death: "Jesus [said], 'Destroy this temple, and in three days I will raise it up.' The Jews then said, 'It has taken forty-six years to build this temple, and will You raise it up in three days?' But He was speaking about the temple of His body. When therefore He was raised from the dead, His disciples remembered that He had said this, and they believed the Scripture and the word that Jesus had spoken" (Jn 2:19–22). "As Jesus was going up to Jerusalem, He took the twelve disciples aside, and on the way He said to them, 'See, we are going up to Jerusalem. And the Son of Man will be delivered over to the chief priests and scribes, and they will condemn Him to death and deliver Him over to the Gentiles to be mocked and flogged and crucified, and He will be raised on the third day'" (Mt 20:17–19).

Friends and foes also agree that Jesus died: "When [the soldiers] came to Jesus and saw that He was already dead, they did not break His legs" (Jn 19:33). "Pilate was surprised to hear that He should have already died. And summoning the centurion, he asked him whether He was already dead. And when he learned from the centurion that He was dead, he granted the corpse to Joseph" (Mk 15:44–45).

Both enemies and disciples agreed that Jesus' body was buried: "Now in the place where He was crucified there was a garden, and in the garden a new tomb in which no one had yet been laid. So because of the Jewish day of Preparation, since the tomb was close at hand, they laid Jesus there" (Jn 19:41–42). To keep everyone honest, the tomb had been sealed: "So they went and made the tomb secure by sealing the stone and setting a guard" (Mt 27:66). On Easter, the soldiers and the chief priests did not question that the body was missing. Also the women and two disciples entered the tomb and saw for themselves that the body was gone (Mt 28:6; Mk 16:6; Lk 24:3; Jn 20:6–8).

There are three conceivable ways by which the body of Jesus could be removed: by His enemies, by His friends, or by Himself.

If His enemies did it, they would have confronted His followers with the body, therefore demonstrating that Jesus was a fraud. They did not. If, as the soldiers were told to say, His disciples removed the body, it would have been a rejection of their

Master. Not only that, they were too afraid to attempt entering the sealed and guarded tomb. When Jesus was captured, they ran off. Peter even denied knowing Jesus—three times. None of His disciples were with Him during the trials before the Sanhedrin and Pilate. At His crucifixion, only John and a few women were at the foot of the cross. Even three days later, they met together "the doors being locked ... for fear of the Jews" (Jn 20:19).

In addition, at Passover the crowds would be ever-present in Jerusalem; the moon would be full; and it is highly unlikely that the entire Roman guard fell asleep at the same time. Sleeping on duty was punishable by death. There is no record of that penalty occurring. Finally, if the soldiers believed that the disciples stole the body, they would have tracked them down and brought them to trial.

Perhaps the most remarkable evidence of the resurrection is the change in the disciples themselves—from cowardice and timidity to courage and boldness. The Book of Acts records again and again how they confronted crowds with sharp accusations and a call to repent and believe. Quoting David, Peter announced in his Pentecost sermon, "He foresaw and spoke about the resurrection of the Christ, that He was not abandoned to Hades, nor did His flesh see corruption" (Acts 2:31).

What kind of a body did Jesus have after He rose from the dead? John informs us that doors and walls did not keep Christ outside the place where the frightened disciples had gathered. He showed them His scars and invited them to feel them. Then "they gave Him a piece of broiled fish, and He took it and ate before them" (Lk 24:42–43). This was not done for nourishment, but to establish the identity of the risen body with the body slain on the cross. The Church through the ages has called the resurrected body "glorified," not bound by time and space. Beyond that we cannot speculate about its nature.

But we can say with confidence that our bodies will also be raised and glorified: "We know that when He appears we shall be like Him, because we shall see Him as He is" (1 Jn 3:2). All the tribulation, trouble, and temptation that make the Lord's Prayer a daily necessity are as nothing. "I consider that the sufferings of this present time are not worth comparing with the glory that is to be revealed to us" (Rom 8:18).

Who Wants Jesus to Die?

Rev. Theodore W. Timler

Ash Wednesday

The Father Wants Jesus to Die

2 Corinthians 5:20–6:2

At the turn of the twentieth century, Morgan Robertson wrote a novel about a ship that sailed between Southampton, England, and the United States. The year was 1898, and it was the ship's third trip from New York to England. The ship, the biggest and grandest liner ever built, never reached its destination. Its hull was ripped open by an iceberg, and it sank with heavy loss of life. The fictional ship was the *Titan*, and the book's title was *Futility*. Fourteen years later on April 15, 1912, this novel was strangely acted out in history in many ironic details. The historical ship was the *Titanic*!

As one looks at the scenes of the Passion history leading to Christ's death, one is struck with a strange paradox, namely, that most persons involved in the story want Jesus to die! God the Father, Satan, Barabbas, the high priest, Pilate, the religious leaders, the crowds, Judas, and Christ Himself—all want Jesus to die! To be sure, there are different agendas, conflicting purposes and motives. Many are selfish, but others catch the unfathomable dimension of God's purpose and goal, the proper, right reason that Christ must die.

Satan Destroyed the Gift of Life and Relationship with the Father

As sad and painful as it must have been, the Father's desire for Christ to die was necessitated by sin and its tragic consequences. God's gift of life at creation was destroyed by Satan through sin, and humankind became alienated from God. There was only one way for that tragedy to be reversed; namely, Christ was made to die as our substitute to pay for the sins of the world. Only then could we have life restored; only then could our relationship with the Father be reconciled. As the second lesson appointed for this Ash Wednesday declares, "We implore you on behalf of Christ, be reconciled to God. For our sake He made Him to be sin who knew no sin, so that in Him we might become the righteousness of God" (2 Cor 5:20b–21).

This action of God reveals the drama that brings victory over death by restoring life. It is a most unconventional and unexpected plan, not accomplished by a show of earthly might and armies but through apparent failure: disciples forsake their leader, betrayal by a close friend, insults and gross injustices, and the human helplessness of Christ, who could prevent it all, saying, "Do you think that I cannot appeal to My Father, and He will at once send Me more than twelve legions of angels?" (Mt 26:53). Yet He doesn't call down the angels and, later, when He is taunted to come down from the cross to prove He is who He claims to be, He doesn't do that either. It looks like a total failure. The hopes and dreams that Christ had inspired in the lives of people were dashed. Yet the war is fought successfully on a different plane with an unconventional procedure—not by the one who lives but by the one who dies! The victory is won by death! The death that the Father desires is the ultimate sacrifice that pays and atones for our sins and reconciles us with God.

Christ was not simply the victim of His environment or circumstances nor was He helpless to avoid death. The Bible affirms that He chose to obey the will of His Father and to die because of His lavish love for us! He says, "I lay down My life that I may take it up again. No one takes it from Me, but I lay it down of My own accord. I have authority to lay it down, and I have authority to take it up again" (Jn 10:17–18). The scenes of Lent are really a glimpse of the cosmic war being waged between God and Satan for our salvation!

The Father loves and cares for us so much that He sent His Son to that cruel, crude death. Why? Because of that supreme, selfless sacrifice on Calvary's cross, sin and death no longer have power over us. What unfathomable love! It is in that context that the Father wants Christ to die.

By the Spirit's power, let this Lent be a time of reflection, appreciation, and recommitment for us as we express our thanks in worship, in obedience, and in trust.

How Christ Must Die

The plan and purpose of Christ's death was to redeem and restore us into a right relationship with the heavenly Father. Satan and his followers, however, desired nothing more than to sidetrack or nullify the Father's plan, which would destroy the gift of restored relationships and make Christ's sacrifice ineffective.

Thanks and praise to our Lord and Savior, Jesus Christ, for the power, the will, the grace, and the love to fulfill this plan of the Father! Gratefully, with the apostle Paul we exclaim, "Oh, the depth of the riches and wisdom and knowledge of God! How unsearchable are His judgments and how inscrutable His ways! . . . For from Him and through Him and to Him are all things. To Him be glory forever" (Rom 11:33, 36).

Next week we will consider another participant from the Passion history of Jesus who says that Jesus must die—Satan himself!

Lent 2

Satan Wants Jesus to Die

Matthew 4:1–11

NASA has an elaborate plan of recovery to prevent potential tragedy in our space program. There are many obstacles to space travel, including the weather, the temperature, the open seas, and gravity. Much money and effort are expended to provide a successful reentry and return to earth and, thus, to ensure safety for the astronauts.

In a spiritual sense, the heavenly Father paid a dear price to initiate successfully a "plan of recovery" for the people whom He created to live in fellowship with Him. He sent His Son, Jesus, to rescue, renew, restore, reconcile, and redeem so that God's original blueprint can be a reality again. Jesus identifies this work in Jn 10:10, "I came that they may have life and have it abundantly."

Today we consider another participant in the Passion story who says Jesus must die—Satan.

Satan Seeks to Interfere

Obviously Satan desires to disrupt, interfere, or otherwise bring God's rescue plan to a screeching halt. He plots to overthrow God's plan of sending Jesus to die the "right" way and for the "right" reason—as the ransom price to redeem lost humankind. Satan will do anything to nullify and neutralize the work of Christ.

In our text, note the anger, anxiety, frustration, and irrational behavior of Satan when he sees his efforts frustrated and destroyed. Christ has entered the arena of human history. The apostle Paul writes in Galatians, "But when the fullness of time had come, God sent forth His Son, born of woman, born under the law, to redeem those who were under the law, so that we might receive adoption as sons" (4:4–5). Moreover, to young Timothy Paul writes, "Christ Jesus . . . abolished death and brought life and immortality to light through the gospel" (2 Tim 1:10) to resolve the demands of the Father's wrath and judgment because of our disobedience. God's holiness and justice insisted on it!

Satan knows who Jesus is. He understands the purpose of Christ's life on this earth and seeks to stifle God's plan to redeem us. In our text, Satan tempts Jesus in order to deceive Him and to distract Him from His mission as Messiah. Thanks to God, Christ successfully withstood Satan's temptations in this cosmic war, enduring human stress and pain as part of His redemptive work and payment for our sins. Heb 4:15–16 says, "For we do not have a high priest who is unable to sympathize with our weaknesses, but one who in every respect has been tempted as we are, yet without sin. Let us then with confidence draw near to the throne of grace, that we may receive mercy and find grace to help in time of need."

One can see the desperate position of Satan, who thought he had successfully thwarted God's plan, only to have Christ win the battle that day! The event of our text and Christ's other victories puts Satan in a position where he cannot stop God's redemptive plan. It is finished! Still, Satan tries to deceive us into ignoring or doubting our faith. In *The Screwtape Letters*, C. S. Lewis masterfully reveals how sneaky, subtle, and insidious Satan is and the ways he attempts to delude humankind. We rejoice that Satan was unable to undermine Christ's determination to be our Redeemer, yet we must be aware of and guard against the schemes Satan uses every day to lead us astray.

In our text, Jesus shows us how to defeat Satan through knowing and using the Word of God properly, to hear both Law and Gospel and effectively apply these tools in our life. This Lenten season is an appropriate time for diligent, disciplined, devotional study of that Word, the only effective tool to provide victory over Satan's temptations, which seek to draw us away from Christ.

Satan's Tactics

Satan tempts Jesus with providing bodily needs, trying to convince Him to jump from the pinnacle of the temple, and offering Him "all the kingdoms of the world and their glory" (Mt 4:8). All Christ has to do is bow down to Satan! These are the deceptions of Satan. He emphasizes gain, glory, and self-aggrandizement to minimize the consequences of ungodly behavior. Satan's tactics are the same today. Satan's temptations notwithstanding, it is of great comfort and power that Christ thwarted each scheme and accomplished what He promised—to save us from sin!

Yes, the Father also wanted Jesus to die, but He wanted it done the right way, at the right time, in the right place, and for the right purpose. The determination of God to shower us with His mercy and grace wins! Although we face temptations to sin, through the power of the Word we can overcome the wiles and will of Satan.

Who wants Jesus to die? Next week—Barabbas.

Lent 3

Barabbas Wants Jesus to Die

Mark 15:6–15

Interwoven in the drama of Christ's Passion is a plot we must seek to understand if we are to grasp fully the depth of God's power and love. Behind the historic scenes of Christ's suffering and death is a cosmic war, a battle between God and Satan. It began when the evil angels fell away from the Almighty and then seduced God's first created man and woman to rebel against God's command. The Bible records other battles, such as the temptations of Jesus in the wilderness and His miracles of casting out demons. The suffering and death of Christ is the final, decisive battle and the turning point for God's victory!

Satan Uses Barabbas

Satan wants Jesus to die so that he, Satan, might control the world and all who dwell therein. He must be careful that Jesus dies for the wrong reason or in a different way from the Father's holy will, which would preclude Jesus as the Savior and render His work useless. Then we would remain in our sin—Satan's ultimate goal. Satan uses others, such as Barabbas, to attempt to achieve his goal.

Satan fanned the self-centered drive in Barabbas. Pontius Pilate, following a custom, released a prisoner at the Passover festival. Barabbas wanted Jesus to die so that he could be set free and not suffer the consequences of his crimes. That was his sole concern. He cared nothing about the innocence of Jesus. He and Pilate were two of a kind. "Pilate, wishing to satisfy the crowd, released for them Barabbas, and having scourged Jesus, he delivered Him to be crucified" (v. 15). How easy it is to seek Christ only insofar as He serves our purposes, gratifies our whims, enhances or advances our causes.

Yet through it all, God's purpose continued to unfold. God allowed Barabbas to be freed. If Christ were freed and Barabbas had died, God's plan would be thwarted, and our sins would not be paid. We would have no Redeemer and would spend eternity in hell. So the Father saw that Christ would die for the right reason, though He had no sin. It is amazing how God uses all things for good! The people's choice of Barabbas accomplishes God's purpose!

Christ Frees Barabbas and Us

There is an ironic twist in this story of Barabbas: he wanted Jesus to die so that he could be set free. That is precisely what Christ accomplished, not only for Barabbas but also for all of us. As we personally see the purpose of Jesus' death, by the power of the Spirit we trust Him as our Savior and celebrate the freedom from sin He provides. Thanks and praise to God that despite Satan's attempts to make the Savior's death null and void, Christ died in the right way at the right time and for the right reason—as our Redeemer.

James C. Whittaker recounts the story of the ordeal and rescue of those who were with Captain Eddie Rickenbacker on an airplane that was lost in the Pacific Ocean during World War II. After twenty-two days adrift at sea, Rickenbacker finally saw an island in the distance. He used his last ounce of energy to row his rubber life raft to the small island. As he was about to beach the raft, a large wave pounded against the raft and took it back out to sea. Exhausted, he slumped in the raft. After a brief time, he realized the raft was moving against the waves. The raft was beached despite the laws of nature, while the captain lay helpless on its floor. He credited God for this miracle! The book is titled *We Thought We Heard the Angels Sing*.

God's hand of divine providence is seen in many ways in the Passion history and in our lives. May we be grateful for God's controlling hand in our life and strengthened in the security it brings.

Besides the Father, Satan, and Barabbas, next week the high priest wants Jesus to die.

Lent 4

The High Priest Wants Jesus to Die

John 18:12–14

At Seawolf Park in Galveston, Texas, are two World War II ships for visitors to board and explore—the destroyer escort USS *Stewart* and a submarine. Ironically, the submarine is not the USS *Seawolf* but a similar submarine from the war, the USS *Cavalla*. The *Seawolf* was sunk off the coast of the Philippines on October 3,

1944; its eighty-two-man crew and seventeen U.S. Army special agents aboard were all killed. The sad and strange truth is that one of our own destroyer escorts, the USS *Rowell*, sank the *Seawolf* with its own depth charges! What a pointless loss of life.

In a spiritual parallel, this was Satan's intent. He wanted Jesus to die uselessly and pointlessly so God's purpose would be thwarted. If that had happened, our sins would not be paid for, and we would face the tortures of hell. This day, consider the intrigue surrounding one of these pointless death attempts of Satan. It involves the high priest.

Wrong Reasons to Die

After Jesus was betrayed, "the band of soldiers and their captain and the officers of the Jews arrested Jesus and bound Him. First they led Him to Annas, for he was the father-in-law of Caiaphas, who was high priest that year. It was Caiaphas who had advised the Jews that it would be expedient that one man should die for the people" (vv. 12–14). The message was correct, but the motive was wrong. Earlier in the Gospel of John, Jesus had raised Lazarus from the grave and many people came to believe in Him. The chief priests and the Pharisees called a meeting of the Sanhedrin. " 'What are we to do? For this man performs many signs. If we let Him go on like this, everyone will believe in Him, and the Romans will come and take away both our place and our nation.' But one of them, Caiaphas, who was high priest that year, said to them, 'You know nothing at all. Nor do you understand that it is better for you that one man should die for the people, not that the whole nation should perish' " (Jn 11:47–50).

The high priest's motive is expedience and perhaps selfishness and even jealousy. The Sanhedrin concluded that the end justified the means. So Caiaphas advised the killing of one man rather than agitating the Romans, who might come and destroy the Jewish hierarchy. There was a delicate balance of toleration. Although these men were religious leaders, they did not understand the purpose of Christ and why He must die. They saw Jesus not as the Messiah but as a rebellious renegade and, potentially, a pawn to exploit for their own advantage.

Christ on My Terms

Today, also, many people seek to use or exploit Christ for their own end or purpose. They want Him on their terms. They pervert the purpose of the Law. They seek salvation in their own performance of the Law and fail to see salvation through Christ alone. They avoid church and anything else that smacks of spiritual commitment. They ask only what Christ can do for them.

Such human selfishness plays into the hands of Satan. We can learn much from Satan's subtle ways for our spiritual living. We constantly need to be on guard, asking, "Who is controlling my life? What is God's plan for me?"

JESUS RESPONDS WITH HEALING

Outside the Garden of Gethsemane was a servant of the high priest. Peter wished to defend Christ from death, so he drew his sword and cut off the ear of the servant. But Christ and the Father knew He must die, so Peter's defense didn't help at all. Jesus told Peter to put away the sword. Ironically, Jesus, whom the high priest sought to kill, healed the priest's servant. Can you imagine how the servant then felt toward Jesus and how he may have questioned the high priest's view of Christ? How it must have changed his values! When we see God's gracious hand at work in our lives, our values also change!

GOD USES THE HIGH PRIEST

Although the high priest had no concept of the profound truth he spoke, he nevertheless gave a precise explanation of why Jesus must die. John records, "He did not say this of his own accord, but being high priest that year he prophesied that Jesus would die for the nation, and not for the nation only, but also to gather into one the children of God who are scattered abroad. So from that day on they made plans to put Him to death" (11:51–53).

God uses the office of the high priest to prophesy the truth about Christ, though the high priest opposes it. God's ways are intriguing and unexpected, but they are always carried out. The Old Testament describes what Christ's death is accomplishing for us. "As far as the east is from the west, so far does He remove our transgressions from us" (Ps 103:12). The apostle Paul says it beautifully, "For if while we were enemies we were reconciled to God by the death of His Son, much more, now that we are reconciled, shall we be saved by His life. More than that, we also rejoice in God through our Lord Jesus Christ, through whom we have now received reconciliation" (Rom 5:10–11). Thank God that Christ died according to God's plan to give us forgiveness of sins and new life, a life that lasts forever.

On then to next week, when we consider Pontius Pilate, who wants Jesus to die.

Lent 5

Pilate Wants Jesus to Die

John 19:10–16

In a tapestry, the various threads all contribute to the ultimate design, beauty, and completeness. So in the Passion history, the threads of different lives weave into the main plot. Everyone wants Christ to die, but each has a different agenda and pur-pose.

PILATE WANTS JESUS TO LIVE

Pilate is different from the other threads in this history in one sense. Initially, Pilate doesn't want Jesus to die. If his motive were compassion, that attitude would be fine, but it is not. Trying to protect Christ from death, ironically, actually stands in the way of God's plan. We see this interest on the part of Pilate in a number of scenes:

1. "Then Pilate said to the chief priests and the crowds, 'I find no guilt in this man'" (Lk 23:4). "Look, nothing deserving death has been done by Him. I will therefore punish and release Him" (Lk 23:15–16).

2. "Pilate addressed them once more, desiring to release Jesus, but they kept shouting, 'Crucify, crucify Him!' A third time he said to them, 'Why, what evil has He done? I have found in Him no guilt deserving death. I will therefore punish and release Him'" (Lk 23:20–22).

3. "While he was sitting on the judgment seat, his wife sent word to him, 'Have nothing to do with that righteous man, for I have suffered much because of Him today in a dream'" (Mt 27:19).

4. "So when Pilate saw that he was gaining nothing, but rather that a riot was beginning, he took water and washed his hands before the crowd, saying, 'I am innocent of this man's blood; see to it yourselves'" (Mt 27:24).

SATAN IS AT WORK

Sparing Jesus' life would thwart God's intention that Christ must die to pay for the sins of the world. So when Pilate tried to postpone death or stop it altogether, he actually fostered Satan's plan. But God ensures that His plan is carried out! As we read in John 18: "Pilate said to them, 'Take Him yourselves and judge Him by your own law.' The Jews said to him, 'It is not lawful for us to put anyone to death.' This was to fulfill the word that Jesus had spoken to show by what kind of death He was going to die" (vv. 31–32). How comforting to know that our God is in control.

Pilate Wants Jesus to Die

Later in our text we see Pilate shifting his position to wanting Jesus to die. Pilate's final consent and desire to have Him die was for his own selfish motive, not to fulfill God's purpose. He wanted to please the crowds so that they would support him. It was an unfortunate death, but necessary for political expedience. Pilate tried to maintain a good self-image and an attitude of self-acceptance by the Jews. If they were displeased, they would send a delegation to Rome to complain to Caesar, as they had done previously. If they were to complain again, Pilate could lose his governorship and risk his political future.

Pilate was so close to Jesus and yet so far. He had the opportunity to talk to Jesus about His death—why He had to die and would allow Himself to be put to death. That would have explained Christ's passive posture. That could have opened a new world for Pilate, but he didn't take the time, he didn't have the interest to see what Christ was about until it was too late.

Despite Pilate, God relentlessly pursued the goal of Good Friday. Scripture clearly proclaims that through the cross, we have reconciliation with the Father, forgiveness of sins, and the promise of eternal life. The writer to the Hebrews declares, "Since therefore the children share in flesh and blood, He Himself likewise partook of the same things, that through death He might destroy the one who has the power of death, that is, the devil, and deliver all those who through fear of death were subject to lifelong slavery" (2:14–15). We rejoice that God is in control and that His will is done despite evil forces such as Pilate. How comforting this is! Fortified with such promises we are able, confidently, to live for Him in peace and joy!

The final character who wants Jesus to die should come as no surprise to any of us: Judas.

Lent 6

Judas Wants Jesus to Die

John 12:4–6

Finally, on this sixth week in Lent, who wants Jesus to die? Judas, of course.

THE WRONG KINGDOM

Our text notes, "But Judas Iscariot, one of His disciples (he who was about to betray him) . . ." (v. 4). Judas seemed to be more perceptive and insightful than the others. He seemed to sense the mood of the day and the movement of events in history. No doubt he remembered the words of Jesus, "See, we are going up to Jerusalem. And the Son of Man will be delivered over to the chief priests and scribes, and they will condemn Him to death and deliver Him over to the Gentiles to be mocked and flogged and crucified, and He will be raised on the third day" (Mt 20:18–19). Judas wondered, Will the attempt to set up a new kingdom fail?

Judas was aware that many believers hoped (erroneously) that Christ's "kingdom" would be an earthly one, perhaps overthrowing the Romans and establishing a kingdom as in the days of David, centered in Jerusalem. That was a common thought.

This attitude prevailed among the eleven other disciples as well. At Christ's ascension they asked, "Lord, will You at this time restore the kingdom to Israel?" (Acts 1:6). Judas saw a need to separate and distance himself from Jesus, and so he made a deal with the religious leaders to betray Him. If Christ must die in the process—so be it!

JUDAS WAS SELF-SERVING

Judas was self-serving at the expense of others. He had a smooth line to cover his motives. His intent was not necessarily to destroy the others out of jealousy, spite, or revenge, but to use them to his advantage. His actions were quick and decisive, though they would result in Jesus' death. This was the inference of the chief priest's comments to him. We see this later when Judas has second thoughts as Jesus' death became imminent. He confessed that he had "sinned by betraying innocent blood" (Mt 27:4). The officials simply said, "What is that to us? See to it yourself" (Mt 27:4). In other words, "Tough!"

Did Judas really catch the full impact of his betrayal and of stealing a little now and then from the treasury? Or did he just get caught up in the moment with an irrational opportunity and not consider the consequence of his actions? The Greek verb for "betraying" implies a process over a period of time, and the "pilfering" was repeated, so it would seem this was a conscious deliberate action on his part, regardless of his conscience. This troubling attitude is rampant today, namely, not being accountable or responsible for or disregarding the consequences.

Left unchecked, sins grow until they become monsters that control our lives. Sin must be dealt with immediately, acknowledging that our action is against God's will and therefore wrong. It is imperative to confess our sin, realizing we are not the one who sets the rules of what is right and what is wrong—God does! Confessing our sins is not the end of the action, because God has given us Christ. Trusting in the power of the Spirit, we have forgiveness!

JUDAS ACCOMPLISHED GOD'S PURPOSE

As ironic as it is, by betraying Jesus to the chief priest, which in turn precipitated Jesus' crucifixion and death, Judas accomplished God's purpose—to have Christ die for us as our substitute and sacrifice. To trust Him as our personal Savior who paid for our sins frees us from our sins. Once we receive the power of God's forgiveness in Christ, we receive the power of Christ. He gives us the desire to resist sin, to be forgiven when we do sin, and to thank God for His restoration. Judas had feelings about Jesus' death, but they were too late, and, unfortunately, his agenda of earthly goals destroyed his faith in Christ as his Redeemer.

Judas was willing for Christ to die to further his own cause. Satan made sure Judas did not see the real purpose of Jesus' death. Give us, O Lord, a deeper appreciation as to why Jesus must die—so we can spend eternity with Him.

Hands of the Savior

Rev. Brian R. Dill

Note: This series may be expanded to include the days of Holy Week. Sermon titles are offered for your creative consideration.

Maundy Thursday: Hands That Consecrate (Matthew 26:26–30)

Good Friday: Hands That Are Pierced (Luke 23:32–46)

Easter: Hands That Prove (John 11:25–27)

Ash Wednesday

Hands That Invite

Matthew 11:28–30

It is not uncommon for us to use our hands to emphasize our speech. I suspect that Jesus gestured with His hands as He spoke, using them as instruments of mercy and love. During this sacred season, we shall view the Passion of our Lord under the overall theme "Hands of the Savior."

One can almost see the hands of the Savior when He spoke these words: *(Gesture)* "Come to Me, all who labor and are heavy laden, and I will give you rest" (Mt 11:28). When we picture that in our minds, we visualize a Savior with open arms and outstretched hands of invitation, smiling to sinners and saying, "Come to Me." But to what does He invite? Why should we welcome the invitation given by the man they call Jesus?

THE BURDEN OF THE LAW

Often when Christ used His hands, He used them to bless someone, for instance, when He blessed the children. Today His invitation is special. He summons you and me! He invites us to be yoked to Himself. He summons all the sinners of this world. He invites us to come to Him for a reason: to place our burdens on Him.

For the people of His day, those burdens were not necessarily the daily stresses of life. They were burdens imposed by their own religious leaders—the burden of earning their own salvation by keeping endless rules, most of which evolved not from God but from religious leaders attempting to cover every contingency God did not specifically address in His Commandments to His people.

In this context the Savior stretches forth His hands and says, "Come to Me . . . and I will give you rest." He was volunteering to take upon Himself the heavy load of their sins. He was willing and able to free those people, encumbered with all those regulations, by obeying the rules in His own life. Our Savior lived His life to perfection. That is a big part in the story of salvation, just as important as the very cross itself.

Now the Savior gestures to you and to me: "Come . . . I will give you rest." He says to us, "I have lived a life that has no flaw; I have done everything necessary to please the Father in heaven for your sake. But I have done even more than that."

We Are Used as Hands of the Savior

"See My hands! Through two thousand years I still use them to summon you to Me. I may even use your hands to be as My hands, embracing the distressed, inviting the doubting, leading little children to hear of My goodness. They are strong hands, for with them I made the world and the universe. I cast the solar systems in place and set in motion all the perfect timing of this endless universe. With these hands I made all of humanity, including you. And even when people determined to walk in the way of sinners, with these hands I embraced them, the untouchables and outcasts.

"With these hands I am inviting you to trust Me for the forgiveness of your sins and to understand that these holy hands were once pierced with spikes on the cross of Calvary. I am inviting you to see these hands and to know in your heart that I suffered and died so you could live forever. My hands were spiked so your hands would be holy.

"I invite you to call upon Me and My strong hands to carry every burden of your life. Your hands cannot carry your burdens, but Mine can and do. These hands—though they are the rough hands of a simple carpenter—will always be hands that invite. They are hands that say forever, 'Come to Me.'"

Lent 2

Hands That Heal

John 9:6–7

The Savior's hands healed people no matter what their affliction—those possessed with demons and other social outcasts, such as lepers or people with fevers that could kill. The hands of the Savior were always healing hands. For the Son of Man came into this world and extended the mercy of the Father to all.

The man born blind was blind in his vision and in his spirit. He did not know his Maker and he did not yet know that his Maker was facing him in the person of the Savior. This story is so significant it occupies the entire ninth chapter of the Gospel of St. John. It was a controversial healing because of a false idea taught by the priests: that a person's blindness or other birth defect was the result of either his or his parents' grievous sin. People still think like this—that when bad things happen it's because God is punishing them for some specific sin. The Savior put aside this myth when He said, "It was not that this man sinned, or his parents, but that the works of God might be displayed in him" (Jn 9:3).

Jesus spit on the ground, made some mud with the saliva, and with His compassionate hands placed the mudpack on the man's eyes. Jesus ordered him to wash in the pool of Siloam and, thus, the blind man regained his vision. Faith led to obedience, and obedience led to healing. The hands of the Savior had given a brother in the flesh an entirely new perspective of life—the ability to see for the first time.

From Physical to Spiritual Vision

Then comes the story of spiritual vision. The man born blind did not know who had healed him. First, he addressed the Savior as "the man called Jesus" (v. 11); then he referred to Jesus as "a prophet" (v. 17). But when questioned by the Pharisees, he insisted that it was Jesus who had healed him. They threw him out of the temple.

Then the Savior asked the man a question we each must address sometime during life: "Do you believe in the Son of Man?" The blind man replied with a question, "Who is He, sir?" And Jesus said, "It is He who is speaking to you." With a grateful heart this man confessed, "Lord, I believe." And he worshiped Jesus (vv. 35–38). He received two great gifts. First, he had his sight restored. Second, he saw Jesus as his God and Redeemer.

To See the Savior

What an amazing parallel to the way we received our spiritual vision. Every person in this world is born with a heart and a soul blind to God. The Savior seeks those who are blind of heart. The Redeemer loves the rebellious of spirit so completely that He would have His healing hands spiked to a cross. That is compelling and divine love.

When His flesh and blood failed Him at His hour of death, Jesus deleted forever the files of our sins. Nor will He ever recycle that file. He wants us to believe that His hands are extended as hands that heal, that touch the retina of our spirit and make us see Him as the one who came to be our brother and Redeemer.

He has cleared my vision; for I was blind, but now I see! I was born blind to my Lord, and so were you. But Christ has given us the sight to see that He is worthy of our praise. For the One whose hands healed the blind man is the same One whose hands were nailed to a Roman cross. And there on that cross, those hands spoke of the love and grace that our heavenly Father has embedded in His heart for sinners great and small.

Lent 3

Hands That Provide

Matthew 14:19–20

The hands of Jesus are hands that invite and hands that heal. They also are hands that provide. The feeding of the five thousand clearly demonstrates this divine truth of God who created all things and provides for them.

When God showed Adam and Eve their home on earth, they saw a magnificent garden with more than enough to feed them and to keep them. As for us, Luther observes in his Small Catechism, "I believe that God has made me and all creatures; that He has given me my body and soul, eyes, ears, and all my members, my reason and all my senses, and still takes care of them" (*Luther's Small Catechism*, p. 15). The hands of the Savior are the hands of God, who bound Himself to provide for all He had made.

The feeding of the five thousand emphasizes that humanity's Savior is also humanity's Maker and Provider. He had no obligation to do what He did. The people He fed were responsible for their situation. They had followed the Savior and forgotten about lunch. Now they were hungry.

The Lord's disciples suggested that the people should pay the price for their lack of foresight. They said, "Send the crowds away" (Mt 14:15). But not Jesus; Jesus provided for them. It is truly amazing that our Lord's hands make up for human failings. In the Garden of Eden, God's creation "bit the hand that fed them," but God decided He would still care for them. He forged a plan to do so—a plan to make them His own!

It is that plan of salvation on which we focus this holy season. Jesus covers our sins and failures and foolish mistakes, just as He fed the multitude who should have brought provisions with them. A boy had a few fish and some bread. Jesus took them, gave thanks, blessed them, and made a great feast.

THE BREAD OF LIFE

The Lord of creation is also our Provider. From His providential hands we have more than just bread for the body; we possess the bread of life, Christ. He tells us to eat this bread—to have Him as part of our being. To be the bread of life for us means to offer us a life of peace with God that is bound in faith to Christ.

Those same hands that made a banquet carried a crossbeam for a Roman cross. Those hands were spiked to that cross, a place of condemnation where true justice would have us hang. Those hands were shown to a doubting Thomas by a risen Lord. And in those scarred hands we behold a Redeemer who provides us with salvation. As He gives us the needs of life, so He provides us, with His divine hands, the means to achieve eternal life.

With the hands that fed a crowd, our Savior prepared a special Meal for us that we cherish and share. By consecrating the bread and wine to be His body and blood, He gave us a new covenant. Whenever we eat this bread and drink this wine, we remember His death until He comes. Jesus is in our heart and mind and understanding. Our body becomes His temple. We dwell in Him because He dwells in us.

Eat His body, drink His blood! It is food of such spiritual value that we shall never die. In the arduous battle of life, we will never go hungry—for we have a Redeemer with hands that provide! Nor will we grow weak from hungry spirits as we fight Satan with all our might.

For Christ is our strength, and Christ is our right. The table is prepared for the family of God to gather to strengthen the resolve of fellowship and the spirit to meet and defeat enemies who would lead us into Satan's kingdom. Jesus defeated this very foe when He said, "Man shall not live by bread alone, but by every word that comes from the mouth of God" (Mt 4:4).

Lent 4

Hands That Pray

Matthew 26:36–45

The hands of the Savior are hands that prayed. This is the focus of today's devotion. If Jesus were God, why did He need to pray? Because He was human. Jesus came to this world as a man, and it was as a man that He carried out His ministry, using His divine powers only to help others and never to make His work of salvation easier for Himself.

COMMUNION WITH THE FATHER

Just as important, for what did our Redeemer pray? First, the hands of Jesus were folded in prayer because, in His humanity, He needed to pray to overcome temptation in every aspect of His life's work. Sometimes we are prone to believe that the only temptations Jesus met and overcame were those three temptations that accompanied His encounter with Satan in the wilderness. But Scripture reminds us that we have "one who in every respect has been tempted as we are, yet without sin" (Heb 4:15). Just like us, Jesus needed strength to meet temptation every day of His life.

Throughout the Word of God, we often read that Jesus went to a distant place to pray. His great, yet so very simple, prayer in the Garden of Gethsemane manifested His agony at its worst. But with hands folded in the act of praying, the Son of God received the required strength and submitted to the will of His Father. He had asked His disciples to watch and pray with Him. But, instead, they slept.

FOCUS

Jesus prayed because He knew His Father was His source of power. How easily it might have been for the man Jesus to take the kingdoms offered Him by Satan. For you and me, the distractions of this world often take our focus from the desire to do the will of the Father. We, too, must pray for such focus. For our nature is to live by the agenda of our human will and not the will of the Father.

In the seventeenth chapter of St. John, Jesus prayed what is called the High Priestly Prayer. It was a prayer of intercession—that His disciples be united in purpose.

To pray for others is an act of unselfish faith. Jesus' prayer for His friends and His enemies is a glowing example of the direction our prayers must take. We are exhorted and encouraged to pray for those in our church as their needs become known to us and for those drifting from the fellowship of the Church that they do not lose the crown of life. The Word of God implores us to pray for civil authorities, regardless of our political affiliations, and to pray for those in need of the knowledge of the saving work of Christ.

PRAY TO FORGIVE

Jesus also prayed for God to forgive His foes. Christ prayed for His enemies even while they were killing Him on the cross. We all were His enemies, lost in sin. His prayer is for us, answered when we come to faith. Now by grace we in turn pray for our enemies, as we are filled with the Spirit of the almighty God. And the Spirit of the Lord comes to us through the means of grace.

Hands folded in prayer are signs of hearts committed. How conscious we are of the Lord's commitment. And knowing that His commitment was to us and for us, shall not each of us, as we view the Savior on the cross this season of Lent, fold our hands in grateful devotion and thanksgiving to God and for purposes like those for which our Lord had His hands folded in prayer to His heavenly Father?

Lent 5

Hands That Resurrect

Matthew 9:19, 23–25

The hands of Jesus have power to raise the dead. If He were not capable of doing this, He would surely not be the God who came to be our Redeemer. But the Son of God is in control of life and death, and He can serve us in life and help us in death.

Death is an enemy of life and an enemy of God. In the reading today, a man of authority came to see Jesus. This man who had civil authority over the Savior came to Him with a plea for mercy. His daughter was dying, and Jesus' reputation had preceded His arrival. Jesus would not refuse.

Responding to the prayer of the ruler, the Son of God determined to use His hands to restore life. The girl was dead. The musicians who gathered at the time of death to cheer the mourners had begun to play. But Jesus would not allow death to claim this victory.

When He told the onlookers that the little girl had not died but was only asleep, they responded with scornful laughter. Leaving the jeering crowd outside, Jesus went into the home. And with hands that raise the dead, He took the little girl by her hand and raised her from death to life.

LIFE IN ALL ITS FULLNESS

This was not the first time He made life. In the beginning our Lord created the heavens and the earth and all living things. Life was the purpose for His coming.

The Lord explained His mission with these words: "I came that they may have life and have it abundantly" (Jn 10:10). He meant a great deal more than inhaling and exhaling breath; rather, He meant to have a heart that was linked to the heart of God. He meant us to have a faith that relied on God. He meant us to have a hope dependent on what God alone can do. He meant us to enjoy life in communion with the Creator and loving fellowship with all creation.

Thus the Lord of life used His hands, which raise the dead, to resurrect a little girl. At the same time, He brought great joy to her father—a ruler of the people. The hands of the Savior brought many blessings to Jews and Gentiles, believers and doubters, faithful and faithless.

Where are you in your relationship with God? Are you alive to God or dead to God—or somewhere in between? The hands of Jesus have raised you from death to life. At your Baptism, it was the hands of Jesus that touched you with His Spirit! When you were brought to church or Sunday School or Christian day school, it was the leading of the Lord. At your confirmation, it was His hand on your head that assured you of life with God. Yes, the hands of the Lord can be found within the hands of many others whose touch can bless us, whether such people know it or not!

When His hands were nailed to the cross, it was really your hands that should have felt the pain! He came to be your substitute. His love for you is beyond human description. It is a love so astonishing that, when you cross the final Jordan, you can be sure that the same hands that raised the little girl from the dead will pull you across the valley of the shadow of death into the blessedness of heaven. For the hands of the Savior have raised you from the death of sin to newness of life.

Lent 6

Hands That Protect

Matthew 14:28

The hands of the Savior are hands that protect. When God made His creatures, He covenanted Himself to protect them. The Maker assumes responsibility for the well-being of the created. The story before us is a great example of hands that protect.

The disciples were in a boat and Jesus came to them, walking on the water. One of those familiar storms had arisen, which could sweep in and out of the lake region in minutes and with little or no warning. It must have been a frightening sight to see Jesus walking on the water. The disciples assumed it was an apparition. So Jesus reassured them, "Take heart; it is I. Do not be afraid" (Mt 14:27). But Peter wanted proof: "Lord, if it is You, command me to come to You on the water" (v. 28). Jesus invited the impetuous Peter to come to Him.

So Peter stepped out of the boat and began to walk on the water toward the Savior. Then the waves and the wind distracted him and he began to sink. But the hands of the Savior are hands that protect. With those mighty hands He reached out to Peter and pulled him to safety. Then Jesus told Peter his faith was lacking. It was! How easy it is for human beings to be distracted by the fearful events of life, to lose our vision of a Lord who promised divine protection to all. Perhaps we are not familiar enough with His Word of promise, or even if we are, we see the winds and waves of life as larger than the grace of our Lord Jesus Christ.

The Protecting Hands of Jesus

Consider the many times when the hands of the Savior were there to protect. He protected the woman caught in the act of adultery from being stoned to death. Jesus did not condone her behavior, but He could not tolerate the hypocrisy of those who stood ready to kill her. He came to bring God's mercy to all sinners. He protected the disciples on other occasions when their lives were in jeopardy. He healed Malchus, the man whose ear Peter cut off in the garden. He even protected Peter from certain death by telling him to sheath his sword, for Peter was greatly outnumbered in the garden at the time Jesus was arrested.

From the cross—though using words, not hands—Jesus protected His mother's future by telling John to take care of her. Also from the cross, He protected the soldiers who put Him there by asking that they be forgiven. And yet again from the cross, He protected a penitent criminal from the worst fate of all—death without God's blessing.

Consider the many times you and I have had Jesus' protection during our lifetimes! He sustained us during the perils of childhood. He prevents the close calls in our vehicles. Our Lord's hands direct the hands of the surgeon to preserve and heal when we are threatened by serious illness. Surely we say with the psalmist, "The Lord is your keeper; the Lord is your shade on your right hand" (Ps 121:5). Indeed, the hands of the Savior protect His creatures.

Protection from the Folly of Sin

But there is a protection we need beyond sickness, injury, or death—the protection we need from the folly of our sin! That is our most dire need. For without protection, without someone to intervene in the health of our soul, there would be consequences eternally damnable! With His hands our Savior carried the cross on which He would die. Our Savior suffered and died for our eternal protection. He who protects us now through the perils of this life has protected us for the purpose of life everlasting. Protection is more than keeping us safe from getting hurt. Its finest form is protection from what will happen to unbelievers on the Last Day.

Consider the confessions you pray in church! When the sign of the cross is made during the Absolution, the hands of the Savior are the hands that are raised! The pastor says, "In the stead and by the command of my Lord Jesus Christ I forgive you all your sins." That is God's eternal reminder that the hands of the Savior have procured a place for us in God's palace! In the world to come we shall be protected eternally in a beautiful, safe, and perfect home.

The hands of the Savior are hands that protect. Do not focus on the fears of life or take your eyes off the waiting Savior. Learn from Peter and learn from Christ! For He stands ready with those same hands to lead us through the valley of the shadow of death and into His visible presence, and we shall dwell in the house of the Lord forever.

Signs of Salvation

Rev. James C. Rogers

Ash Wednesday
The Sign of Ashes
Jeremiah 6:26

The prophet Jeremiah began his ministry around the year 626 BC. His was a thankless task, at least initially, for he was to call the people of Judah to account for their sins and tell them of the disaster that was coming upon them as a result of their wickedness. He describes their sins in the opening chapters of his book. The basic sin was unfaithfulness. This unfaithfulness was true of the prophets, the priests, and the people alike. In the early chapters of Jeremiah, God speaks to His people through Jeremiah with words such as these: "Has a nation changed its gods? . . . My people have changed their glory for that which does not profit. . . . My people have committed two evils: they have forsaken Me, the fountain of living waters, and hewed out cisterns for themselves, broken cisterns that can hold no water. . . . As a thief is shamed when caught, so the house of Israel shall be shamed: they, their kings, their officials, their priests, and their prophets, who say to a tree, 'You are my father,' and to a stone, 'You gave me birth.' For they have turned their back to Me, and not their face. But in the time of their trouble they say, 'Arise and save us!' " (Jer 2:11, 13, 26–27).

THE SIGN OF SACKCLOTH AND ASHES

For centuries, sackcloth and ashes have been signs of sorrow and mourning. Jeremiah says the people should be mourning over their impending destruction, their sins, and their unfaithfulness. History records that Jeremiah's prophecy was fulfilled. Not many years later, the Babylonians swept into Judea from the north, laid siege to Jerusalem, and eventually destroyed Jerusalem and the temple—all because of the people's unfaithfulness.

Are we so different? The people of Israel were trusting in false gods of wood and stone. We are more sophisticated than that, for we trust in the wood of our houses or the stones of our jewelry. Or perhaps more often we trust in the false gods of money markets and mutual funds. The people of Israel forsook God, the spring of living water, and dug their own cisterns, broken cisterns that could not hold water. We, too, have dug cisterns that cannot hold water, for we so often put our trust not in God but in ourselves and in our own accomplishments. Jeremiah accused the people of turning their backs on the Lord—until they were in trouble. Then they would cry out, "Arise and save us!" They paid attention to God only when it was convenient or especially expedient. How much attention do we pay to God? How regularly do we communicate with Him? Do we do it daily, or do we ignore God until trouble comes and we need Him?

It is interesting that Jeremiah does not accuse the people of lying or stealing or cheating or killing or committing adultery; their sin was one of not giving their total allegiance to God, of putting trust in things other than the Lord alone. We do not need to be into lying, stealing, cheating, killing, or committing adultery in order to stand in need of repentance. Perhaps our sins do not involve our actions as much as our attitudes—our attitudes toward God: our "I can take Him or leave Him" attitude; our "I'll worship if it's convenient and if it doesn't interfere with my other activities" attitude; our "Oh, I believe in God, but this area of my life is none of His business" attitude; our "Sure, I believe in Jesus, but everybody knows that if you want to get to heaven, you'd better follow the Golden Rule and live a better-than-average life" attitude; our "God helps those (and only those) who help themselves" attitude. If any of that describes our attitude, God is saying to us, "O . . . My people, put on sackcloth, and roll in ashes" (Jer 6:26). If that is our attitude, sorrow over our sin, for sin still leads to destruction!

Death, the Destroyer

The verse from Jeremiah continues, "O daughter of my people, put on sackcloth, and roll in ashes; make mourning as for an only son, most bitter lamentation, for suddenly the destroyer will come upon us" (Jer 6:26). The ultimate destroyer is death. The imposition of ashes reminds us that we are dust and unto dust we shall return. Death is a tragic, ultimate result of our sinfulness. If we were not sinful, we would not die; but we are sinful, and we will die. It is that simple! Jeremiah says that realization should move us to put on sackcloth and roll in ashes, to mourn with bitter wailing, as if we had lost our only son.

This is Ash Wednesday, the first day of Lent, which culminates on Good Friday. Then, God the Father did in fact lose His only Son. On Good Friday, God the Father must have put on sackcloth and rolled in ashes as His Son hung there on the cross, not for His Son—for His sacrifice was the Father's plan for salvation—but rather for what caused the cross: sinful actions and attitudes of all humankind. Mourning and sorrow marked those six hours that Friday in heaven, while hell rejoiced. But on Easter Sunday, the tables were turned. For on Easter, the destroyer was destroyed; death was defeated.

Thanks Be to God for the Victory over Death

Not that death does not happen anymore, it does; it still serves as a grim reminder of our sin. Death happens, but it no longer destroys. For as St. Paul says, "The sting of death is sin, and the power of sin is the law. But thanks be to God, who gives us the victory through our Lord Jesus Christ" (1 Cor 15:56–57). Jesus came in fulfillment of this prophecy from Isaiah: "The Spirit of the Lord GOD is upon Me, because the LORD has anointed Me to bring good news to the poor; He has sent Me to bind up the brokenhearted . . . to comfort all who mourn . . . to give them a beautiful headdress instead of ashes, the oil of gladness instead of mourning, the garment of praise instead of a faint spirit" (Is 61:1–3).

We who gather around the Lord's Table this day to receive the bread and wine and the body and blood of Christ receive His forgiveness and strength for new life. And later today, when you wash the ashes off your forehead, remember the water of your Baptism, which initially brought you into God's kingdom and connected you to Christ. As the ashes disappear, remember the forgiveness that is yours in Jesus.

Lent 2

The Sign of the Rainbow

Genesis 9:13

No matter how young or old you are, and no matter how many times you have seen one, to behold a rainbow is always an awesome sight.

Maybe you remember from school that rainbows appear when light from the sun strikes a collection of raindrops and that the beautiful colors in the rainbow are caused by the refraction and internal reflection of light rays that enter the raindrops. A bright, full rainbow is indeed a beautiful sight.

THE RAINBOW AS A SIGN OF THE COVENANT

The rainbow is first mentioned in the Bible in Genesis 9, right after the flood in the days of Noah. Noah and his family and all the animals had left the ark. Noah then built an altar and offered a sacrifice to God, and God responded:

"Behold, I establish My covenant with you and your offspring after you, and with every living creature that is with you, the birds, the livestock, and every beast of the earth with you, as many as came out of the ark; it is for every beast of the earth. I establish My covenant with you, that never again shall all flesh be cut off by the waters of the flood, and never again shall there be a flood to destroy the earth." And God said, "This is the sign of the covenant that I make between Me and you and every living creature that is with you, for all future generations: I have set My bow in the cloud, and it shall be a sign of the covenant between Me and the earth. When I bring clouds over the earth and the bow is seen in the clouds, I will remember My covenant that is between Me and you and every living creature of all flesh. And the waters shall never again become a flood to destroy all flesh. When the bow is in the clouds, I will see it and remember the everlasting covenant between God and every living creature of all flesh that is on the earth." God said to Noah, "This is the sign of the covenant that I have established between Me and all flesh that is on the earth." (Gen 9:9–17)

"Never again," God said—three times. Never again would He destroy all life with a flood. Every time He sees a rainbow—the handiwork of His own design— He remembers His promise. And while we see a rainbow only occasionally, God must see a rainbow every day, for there is surely a rainbow somewhere in the world every day.

WHY GOD GRIEVED

Did God regret sending the flood? We walk on thin ice when we try to peer into the mind of God, for we see Him only from a human perspective because we are human. When we talk about Him—indeed, when He talks about Himself—we do it and He does it in human terms, for those are the only terms we can understand. Did God regret sending the flood? Was He sorry He did it? No, but the text does say that God did grieve the fallenness of humankind from His created holiness to the depravity of sin. These verses from chapter 6 of Genesis—just before God sent the flood—are haunting:

> The LORD saw that the wickedness of man was great in the earth, and that every intention of the thoughts of his heart was only evil continually. And the LORD was sorry that He had made man on the earth, and it grieved Him to His heart. (Gen 6:5–6)

The flood was a result of the sinfulness of humanity. After the flood, it was as though God began anew with Noah and his wife and their three sons and their wives—eight people to whom God said (even as He had said to Adam and Eve in the Garden of Eden), "Be fruitful and multiply, teem on the earth and multiply in it" (Gen 9:7).

So He set the rainbow in the sky as a sign of His promise never again to destroy the earth with a flood—no more, no less. Interestingly, God does not say the rainbow would serve as a reminder to man; it would serve as a reminder to Himself. He says, "I will see it and remember the everlasting covenant" (Gen 9:16). But do you know what? Throughout the Old Testament period, when God saw a rainbow, not only did He remember His promise not to destroy the earth with a flood, that temporary fix for sin, but I suspect that every time He saw a rainbow, He also remembered that the permanent solution for sin would be to send His only Son to suffer and die.

The Ultimate Payment for Sin

We are told that before the flood God's heart was filled with pain when He saw that man's heart was filled with evil. Imagine the pain in His heart after the flood when He saw that man's heart was still filled with evil, knowing that the ultimate solution for sin would be the death of His Son. Imagine the pain in His heart when He saw Noah fall into sin. Imagine the pain in His heart when He saw the tower of Babel being built. Imagine the pain in His heart when later in the Old Testament He saw His people Israel continually rebel and worship other gods. Imagine the pain in His heart when He saw His only Son hanging on the cross, suffering for all those sins. But Jesus not only suffered for the sins that had already been committed, He also suffered for all the sins that would be committed. He suffered for the sins that you and I would commit, do commit, and will commit. Imagine the pain in God's heart when we, knowing what Jesus has done for us, continue to sin.

But thanks be to God, the love in God's heart is stronger than the pain in His heart, so that our sin results not in a flood of judgment, but rather in a flood of forgiveness—a flood of forgiveness that came to us in the waters of Baptism, a flood of forgiveness that comes to us in the bread and the wine of the Lord's Supper.

Today, when God sees a rainbow, He still remembers His promise not to destroy the earth with a flood. More so, He also remembers that ultimate solution for sin—the suffering and death of His Son. He remembers it not with pain in His heart, for that Son is now at His right hand, ruling all things for the Church, as St. Paul puts it (Eph 1:22). And what shall we remember when we see a rainbow? The next time you see a rainbow, see it as a sign of salvation. Be reminded that God's final solution for sin was not a flood, but a Savior.

Lent 3

The Sign of the Baby

Luke 2:12

Last week the focus was the sign of the rainbow after the flood in the days of Noah. God set the rainbow in the sky as a sign of His promise never again to destroy the earth with a flood. We said that the flood was a temporary fix for the permanent problem of sin. Throughout the Old Testament period, when God saw a rainbow, not only did He remember His promise not to destroy the earth with a flood, but He also remembered what the permanent solution for sin would be—sending His only Son to suffer for the sin of the entire world. The sign of salvation upon which we focus today is a sign that the fulfillment of that divine plan was about to take place. We read about this sign in Luke 2. One night outside of Bethlehem an angel appeared to some shepherds. The angel told them of the arrival of the Savior, who was Christ the Lord. The angel said, "This will be a sign for you: you will find a baby wrapped in swaddling cloths and lying in a manger" (Lk 2:12).

For the sign of the Savior, the sign of salvation, was not a priest, it was not a prophet, it was not a king, it was not an expert in the Law, it was not a soldier, it was not a politician, it was not an angel—it was a baby.

WHY A BABY?

When God decided to send the ultimate solution for sin, why did He send a baby? After all, Jesus didn't begin His public ministry until He was around 30 years old. That ministry lasted only about three years. Then He was put to death. What purpose did the first twenty-seven years or so of Jesus' life serve? Why did He have to begin life as a baby? God certainly could have sent a 30-year-old man from heaven to earth. After all, when God made Adam and Eve, He did not create two babies. He created two adults. But when God sent the Savior, He sent a baby—a tiny, helpless, crying baby.

JESUS EXPERIENCED OUR LIFE

Thus it is significant that the sign of salvation shared with the shepherds was the sign of a baby. The Savior entered this world as one of us. "When the fullness of time had come, God sent forth His Son, born of woman, born under the law, to redeem those who were under the law, so that we might receive adoption as sons," wrote St. Paul to the Christians in Galatia (Gal 4:4–5). As a baby, Jesus took His place among us and experienced our life completely. "He had to be made like His brothers in every respect, so that He might . . . make propitiation for the sins of the people," says the author of the Epistle to the Hebrews (2:17), and that He might "sympathize with [us in] our weaknesses" (4:15), he says a little later. Then he encourages us, "Let us then with confidence draw near to the throne of grace, that we may receive mercy and find grace to help in time of need" (4:16).

"This will be a sign for you: you will find a baby," the angel said to the shepherds. God the Father gave up His almighty, all-powerful, eternal Son. He gave Him up for us all—as a baby, subject to all the dangers and hazards of humanity, knowing full well what awaited Him here on earth. For God the Father, Christmas must have been as difficult as Good Friday. Such was His love for us. What a sign of salvation that little baby was!

Lent 4

The Sign of Healing

John 4:46–54

This was not the first time Jesus had visited the little village of Cana. In fact, next week's focus in this series will be His first visit there. That visit is alluded to in our text, as John reminds us that it was "where He had made the water wine" (Jn 4:46). John had called that miracle "the first of His signs" (Jn 2:11). Today, we talk about what John calls "the second sign that Jesus did" (Jn 4:54)—the sign of healing.

THE PURPOSE OF MIRACULOUS SIGNS

At least twice St. Matthew describes the ministry of Jesus as consisting of three things: teaching, preaching, and healing. Dozens of healings are recorded in the four Gospels, yet toward the end of his Gospel account the apostle John writes: "Jesus did many other signs in the presence of the disciples, which are not written in this book" (Jn 20:30).

"Signs," John called them. What is the purpose of a sign? A sign does not exist for its own sake; it always points to something beyond itself. That includes the sign of healing. What was the purpose? John continues: "Jesus did many other signs in the presence of the disciples, which are not written in this book; but these are written so that you may believe that Jesus is the Christ, the Son of God, and that by believing you may have life in His name" (Jn 20:30–31). However, it is not accurate to say simply that Jesus healed people so that they would believe. In fact, in our text today Jesus expresses frustration with people who believe only as a result of miraculous signs. Irritated, He says, "Unless you see signs and wonders you will not believe" (Jn 4:48). Note that John does not say that Jesus performed signs so that people would believe; rather, he says that he recorded them—he wrote them down—so that people would believe.

THE SIGN OF HEALING IS A SIGN OF COMPASSION

The sign of healing was not to elicit faith. Rather, the sign of healing was a sign of Jesus' caring, a sign of His compassion. Jesus was concerned about people. In our text today the royal official says, "Sir, come down before my child dies" (Jn 4:49). And Jesus responds by saying, "Your son will live" (Jn 4:50). Jesus fully understood the pain involved when a father sees his son suffer or die. So Jesus intervened and saved the child from death. Permit me to repeat for emphasis what I just said:

Jesus fully understood the pain involved when a father sees his son suffer or die. Do you suppose that perhaps—just maybe—when this distraught father came to Jesus begging for help, when this father fell on his knees and pleaded, "Come down before my child dies," when Jesus was filled with compassion that moved Him to action—do you suppose that Jesus thought of the time when a few months later on a Friday afternoon His own Father would suffer the pain of the death of His Son?

God's Ultimate Sign of Compassion

The cross is God's ultimate sign of caring and compassion! If healing is a sign of caring and compassion, how much more is the Father's willingness to watch His Son die and the Son's willingness to suffer death on the cross? "Come down before my child dies," the official cried out to Jesus. "If You are the Son of God, come down from the cross" (Mt 27:40), the Jewish leaders taunted Jesus on Good Friday. What a temptation that must have been—not only for Jesus to save Himself but also for Him to save His Father the pain of seeing His only Son die.

But the love of the Father and the love of the Son for us were such that Jesus did not come down from that cross. Isaiah had prophesied, "He was wounded for our transgressions; He was crushed for our iniquities; upon Him was the chastisement that brought us peace, and with His stripes we are healed" (Is 53:5). We are healed of the most terrible disease of all—the disease called sin—through Jesus' suffering and death.

Having spoken that primary truth of the Gospel of God's grace, I do not wish only to spiritualize the sign of healing today. To the contrary, the Jesus who healed so many people of physical illnesses during His earthly ministry because He cared, still cares. Our loving Lord cares not only about our souls but about our bodies and spirits as well. That does not mean to imply that He always heals physical diseases exactly when and in the way we desire. But in power and love, He still can and does heal infirmities of mind and body and spirit. "I am the LORD, your healer," God said as early as the Book of Exodus (15:26). "He heals the brokenhearted and binds up their wounds," the psalmist says (147:3). God still heals because He still cares.

There is an interesting phrase in our text today. When Jesus told the father, "Your son will live," John tells us that the man took Jesus at His word and departed. "As he was going down, his servants met him and told him that his son was recovering" (Jn 4:51). "As he was going down," says John. Imagine what it was like for that father as he traveled home. John says he took Jesus at His word. However, imagine his thoughts as he walked the long journey before his servants met him and told him the good news. Imagine his hopes, his dreams, his doubts, and his fears "as he was going down."

Perhaps some of you are still on the way this very hour. Perhaps you, like this desperate father, have asked Jesus for help with a broken spirit or with broken

111

health. You, like that father, have hopes and dreams but also doubts and fears—not knowing for sure what the future holds for you or your loved one.

If that is where you are today, remember that Friday afternoon when a Father watched His Son die for you! Be assured, without a shadow of doubt, of His love, His care, and His compassion.

Lent 5

The Sign of Celebration

John 2:11

It might seem strange that for His first miraculous sign Jesus chose to make 150 gallons of wine at the wedding of an unknown couple in an obscure village in Galilee. Yet He did, and there was a strong response to it. Jesus' disciples responded with faith, as the text notes (v. 11). The master of the banquet responded with surprise, evidenced by his conversation with the bridegroom (v. 10). The bridegroom probably responded with confusion, not knowing exactly what was happening. And though John does not mention this specifically, I suspect there were more than a few wedding guests who were upset that after this miracle, there was no more water for ceremonial washing.

CEREMONIAL WASHING

Ceremonial washing was extremely important among the Jews in those days, especially in Galilee, where there were plenty of Gentiles with whom a Jewish person could come into contact. If you were a Jew and you accidentally touched a Gentile, you poured water over your hands to make them ceremonially clean again. If you went shopping in the marketplace, you washed your hands when you got home, for you had probably touched some items made by or at least touched by a Gentile, which made you ceremonially unclean. There were also rules about the ceremonial washing of plates, cups, and bowls, and even tables and chairs. These rules about ceremonial washing were not based on the Bible, but on what was called the traditions of the elders. It was not unusual for a large crowd of people to be present at a wedding feast, which often lasted for several days. So the host of the party had made sure that there was plenty of water, properly stored, for the ritual washings that might be necessary as the people would come and go during the course of the wedding feast. And what does Jesus do? He orders that the six large containers, which had held the water for the ceremonial washing, be filled with water. Perhaps they had been full at the beginning of the feast, but now they were far less than full. They were filled up again. Then, as the water is drawn from the jars, it has become wine.

THE CELEBRATION CONTINUES

The result of the miracle was twofold. On the one hand, there could be no more ceremonial washings. On the other hand, the celebration could continue. That is significant. Jesus was not interested in ceremonial washings or in the traditions of the elders. Jesus came so that people could celebrate. "I came that they may have life and have it abundantly," He said in Jn 10:10. To those who were critical of His lifestyle, Jesus responded, "John [the Baptizer] came neither eating nor drinking, and they say, 'He has a demon.' The Son of Man came eating and drinking, and they say, 'Look at Him! A glutton and a drunkard, a friend of tax collectors and sinners!'" (Mt 11:18–19). Jesus came so that people could celebrate.

If it seems strange that for His first miraculous sign Jesus chose to make 150 gallons of wine at the wedding of an unknown couple in an obscure village in Galilee so that a good celebration might continue, it may also seem strange that our focus for this day is on celebration. After all, we are in the season of Lent. And perhaps it is a bit strange. Celebration is not normally a posture for the way in which we worship during these weeks of repentance. Garrison Keillor, who takes delight in chiding us Lutherans, says that Lutherans live like Lent lasts all year long. Is there any truth to that? We Lutherans talk about "celebrating" Holy Communion, for example. But if a stranger walked in during the time when we are receiving the Sacrament, would he recognize it as a celebration? Perhaps, perhaps not, but it is a celebration: a celebration of sins forgiven, a celebration of eternal life assured, a celebration of faith strengthened. I am not suggesting that we skip and laugh our way to the altar of our Lord, but it is also important to remember that this bread and wine, this body and blood of Christ, is a sign of life, not death. The Lord's Supper is a foretaste of heaven itself!

You and I, as the people of God, have reason to celebrate! We can live with freedom and joy—in contrast to the old way of slavery to the Law. The Law was symbolized by the ceremonial washings that Jesus replaced in the course of the miracle at the wedding in Cana, the miracle John calls His first "sign." This first sign was a sign of celebration—a celebration that will continue for all eternity in heaven, but which can start here and now.

Jesus began His ministry with a sign of celebration as He made water into wine, allowing a celebration to continue. Interestingly, wine was also involved at the end of that ministry. For in John 19 we read, "After this, Jesus, knowing that all was now finished, said (to fulfill the Scripture), 'I thirst.' A jar full of sour wine stood there, so they put a sponge full of the sour wine on a hyssop branch and held it to

His mouth. When Jesus had received the sour wine, He said, 'It is finished,' and He bowed His head and gave up His spirit" (vv. 28–30).

At that moment, the devil and all his angels began to celebrate. But their celebration was short-lived, because several hours later, Jesus showed up—alive—and announced that their party was over. For His words "It is finished" did not mean the end of His life but the completion of His mission, namely, to pay the price of sin with His own life and death. The celebration then moved from hell to heaven as the angels there began to celebrate. And as word of His resurrection became known, His followers began to celebrate here on earth. That celebration continues today and will continue forever. Let's join in the celebration—even during these days of Lent, indeed, especially during these days of Lent.

Lent 6

The Sign Spoken Against

Luke 2:34

Three weeks ago the sign of salvation was the sign of a baby, based on Lk 2:12. On the night of Jesus' birth the angel told the shepherds, "This will be a sign for you: you will find a baby wrapped in swaddling cloths and lying in a manger" (Lk 2:12). Today, our sign is based on another verse from that same chapter. Jesus was 40 days old and His parents took Him to the temple in Jerusalem "to present Him to the Lord" (Lk 2:22), as the Law required for firstborn sons. You remember the story. An elderly, pious man by the name of Simeon was in the temple that day. The Holy Spirit had revealed to Simeon that this 6-week-old baby was the Messiah. Simeon took the child in his arms and praised God with words that have come to be known as the Nunc Dimittis: "Lord, now You are letting Your servant depart in peace, according to Your word; for my eyes have seen Your salvation that You have prepared in the presence of all peoples, a light for revelation to the Gentiles, and for glory to Your people Israel" (Lk 2:29–32). Luke tells us "His father and His mother marveled at what was said about Him" (Lk 2:33).

Then, according to the next verses (vv. 34–35), "Simeon blessed them and said to Mary His mother, 'Behold, this child is appointed for the fall and rising of many in Israel, and for a sign that is opposed (and a sword will pierce through your own soul also), so that thoughts from many hearts may be revealed.'"

A Prophecy Fulfilled

Mary and Joseph must have shuddered when they heard those ominous words. "A sign that is opposed." That prophecy was certainly fulfilled. In Luke's Gospel alone we see Jesus spoken against many, many times. At the very beginning of His ministry Jesus spoke in the synagogue in Nazareth—the town in which He spent His boyhood years. At first, the hometown crowd was amazed at the authority that marked Jesus' teaching. But when Jesus' words begin to hit a little too close to home, Luke tells us, "All in the synagogue were filled with wrath" (Lk 4:28). They were so enraged that they drove Him out of town and wanted to throw Him off the edge of a cliff. But Jesus escaped. Imagine the talk in Nazareth in the days that followed. Imagine how He must have been spoken against!

Later in Luke's Gospel a man who was paralyzed was brought to Jesus. Jesus tells the man that his sins were forgiven. The Pharisees and the teachers of the law accuse Him of blasphemy (Lk 5:17–21). A little later they speak against Jesus because He and His disciples did not fast (Lk 5:33). In the next chapter they speak against Him because He and His disciples pluck some ears of grain on the Sabbath (Lk 6:1–2). That same day Jesus heals a man whose right hand was shriveled. They condemn Him for healing on the Sabbath, and Luke concludes this chapter, "They were filled with fury and discussed with one another what they might do to Jesus" (Lk 6:11). Jesus was indeed a sign spoken against.

When a sinful woman anointed Jesus' feet with perfume, they speak against Him and say, "If this man were a prophet, He would have known who and what sort of woman this is who is touching Him, for she is a sinner" (Lk 7:39). In the next chapter even Jesus' mother and brothers get into the act. They thought He was going off the deep end and wanted to talk some sense into Him (Lk 8:19–21). There were some who accused Jesus of casting out demons through the power of the prince of demons (Lk 11:15). Later, when Jesus heals a crippled woman on the Sabbath, the ruler of the synagogue becomes indignant and speaks against Jesus to anyone who would listen (Lk 13:10–14). Luke tells us, "The tax collectors and sinners were all drawing near to hear Him. And the Pharisees and the scribes grumbled, saying, 'This man receives sinners and eats with them' " (Lk 15:1–2). Jesus was indeed a sign spoken against.

And we all know what happened at the end of Jesus' life. His disciple Judas joined in the plot against Him. At Jesus' trial—first before the high priest and then before Pontius Pilate—all kinds of false witnesses were brought forward to speak against Him. Even Peter spoke against Him as he denied Him. When He was on the cross, they continued to speak against Him—mocking and jeering. Even the criminals who were crucified with Him joined in speaking against Him!

How Do We Speak about Jesus?

"This child [will be] . . . a sign that is opposed" (Lk 2:34), Simeon had prophesied. How true it was. His hometown people, the members of His family, the Pharisees, the experts in the law, the high priest, the Jewish leaders, the Roman authorities, the Roman soldiers, the disciples, the criminals crucified with Him—all spoke against Jesus.

How do we speak about Jesus? What do we say about Him? We would not be here if we intentionally speak against Jesus. Most of us would probably admit that we do not speak very much about Him at all. But do we ever speak His name in vain? Are the terms "Jesus" and "Christ" used by us in positive ways or are they sometimes used as expletives? If we speak His name recklessly, we are actually speaking against Him! If we are involved in a conversation about religion and the tenor of the conversation is that all religions are the same and it doesn't make any difference what you believe so long as you believe, do we speak up for Jesus, who is the way, the truth, and the life? Or do we speak against Him with our silence? When an opportunity to share our faith with a friend or relative presents itself, and we change the subject, we are in fact speaking against Jesus with our silence. And it is true that actions often speak louder than words. What do we say about Jesus with our daily lives? If our daily lives do not reflect our Christian faith, then we are speaking against Christ with our actions.

Jesus still is being spoken against—not just by atheists, not just by the irreligious, and not just by enemies of the Church. Sadly, He is sometimes spoken against by us. Sometimes we speak against Him with our words. Sometimes we speak against Him with our silence. And sometimes we speak against Him with our actions and our attitudes.

There Is Forgiveness

The apostle John says in one of his letters:

> If we say we have no sin, we deceive ourselves, and the truth is not in us. If we confess our sins, He is faithful and just to forgive us our sins and to cleanse us from all unrighteousness. If we say we have not sinned, we make Him a liar, and His word is not in us. My little children, I am writing these things to you so that you may not sin. But if anyone does sin [and now listen carefully to this], we have an advocate with the Father, Jesus Christ the righteous. (1 Jn 1:8–2:1)

Imagine that! When we sin—including our sins of speaking against Jesus—Jesus speaks up for us! "Father, forgive them," He says, "they know not what they do" (Lk 23:34). "Father, forgive them," He says, "for I have already suffered the punishment for those sins." "Father, forgive them," He says, "for they are My friends, and I laid down My life for them."

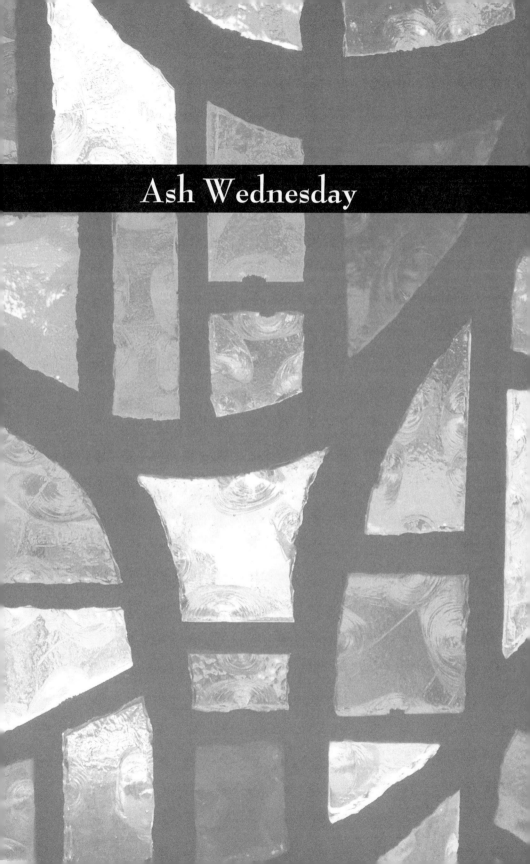

Ash Wednesday

Rend Your Hearts

Joel 2:12–14

The Mardi Gras celebration just passed is a wild party, full of excess, before the Lenten season begins. But Mardi Gras is not high on the list of festivals I would care to attend. If I were wanting one last blowout before the season of Lent, I would prefer Shrove Tuesday. A celebration that originated in Britain, it is also known as Pancake Day. As a pancake lover, that's my kind of celebration.

The London suburb of Olney has held a pancake race every Shrove Tuesday since 1445. That year, a housewife, dashing to get to church on time, arrived at the service still clutching her frying pan with a pancake in it. Today, Olney housewives, attired in head scarfs and aprons, dash with a frying pan and a pancake from a pub in the city square to the Church of St. Peter and St. Paul. Then everyone enjoys copious servings of pancakes, sausage, and the works—the last indulgence until Easter.

Through the ages, Lent has become a time for fasting and for giving up things—denying ourselves something we enjoy. Perhaps the idea of denial is not the reason, but Lent is no longer the holy season it once was. Mardi Gras is still popular, but that's a party. Lent is not a season that we anticipate!

A TIME FOR PEACE

In our text, the prophet Joel suggests that giving up something is not the purpose of Lent at all. Although the Lord speaks of "fasting, with weeping, and with mourning" (Joel 2:12), the real focus is "return to Me with all your heart. . . . rend your hearts and not your garments" (vv. 12–13). Lent's real purpose is not to deny, but to admit. To repent. "Return to the LORD, your God" (v. 13), says Joel. We are invited to bring our sins and lay them before the throne of God. What Lent asks us to "give up" is not meat or candy or television, but our guilt and our anguish—our gloom and our despondency. Lent should be a time of personal peace, a time when we deal with the guilt that burdens us and destroys our joy.

After the Loma Prieta earthquake in 1989, many children needed intensive counseling. One child refused to close any door. If someone else did, it was okay, but he would not! Counselors discovered that his mother had repeatedly told him not to slam the door, which he did whenever he wanted her attention. The day of the earthquake, precisely when it struck, he had slammed the door—causing, he thought, the ground to shake, the house to tilt, and the china cabinet to fall over.

He became traumatized. He believed he was guilty of the earthquake. Irrational, but very real to him.

We often hear of people who can carry their guilt for sins or crimes no longer and confess years later—or ask for forgiveness or make restitution. The IRS receives an envelope filled with cash. A man confesses to a killing for which another man has already been convicted and jailed. Why? "I can't get it off my mind," he explains. Sometimes we are troubled and don't know why. It may be unresolved guilt. It may be the need to say, "I'm sorry." Lent is the time to deal with these difficulties. For some it is helpful to deny desires for alcohol or chocolate, but for all of us, it is a time to admit our faults—a time of repentance, a time to rend our hearts, a time for concern about what we think and say and do.

A TIME FOR ABSOLUTION

Not only is Lent a time for confession, it is also a time for absolution. "Return to the LORD, your God," says Joel, "for He is gracious and merciful, slow to anger, and abounding in steadfast love." We need absolution, because it does no good to confess if we still blame ourselves. This may be the reason many people don't like the emphasis of the Lenten season. They never let go of their sin. They hold on to it. They keep dragging it around, worrying about it, living with it. They never put their sin aside and move on. They never experience absolution and forgiveness. A wise man I knew said, "The devil has two lies he uses all the time. The first he tells us before we sin that one little sin doesn't really matter. The second he tells us after we sin—that now we are worthless and hopeless." They are both lies. Lent is a time for repentance—and absolution.

Lent is also a time for renewal. It is a time to turn our burdens over to Christ and allow Him to carry them for us. Marc Chagall's painting *The Sacrifice of Isaac* depicts Abraham as he prepares to plunge a knife into the heart of his young son, Isaac: An angel has seized his hand and holds it. At the side of the altar, a ram is caught by its horns in the bushes, showing that God provided a sacrifice to take the boy's place. In an upper corner of the painting, Chagall placed another figure— Jesus carrying His cross to Golgotha.

That corner is our focus during Lent—Jesus. God's Son took our sin, our guilt, and carried it to Calvary, where He died in our place so we can be forgiven and have new life. That's why we need Lent. We are invited by God during this wonderful season to repent, to be absolved by Him, and to turn our burdens over to Christ. More than a time to deny ourselves what we most enjoy, Lent is a time to know the true joy of living.

Rev. Wayne R. Viereck

Treasures of the Heart

Matthew 6:16–21

Wonder with me how we are to obey our Lord's words for this hour on this day. This is, after all, Ash Wednesday—a day of somberness, sometimes evidenced by a display of ashes on our forehead. Such a ritual may serve as a witness to faith, a way of showing others that I am a Christian and that our Savior's death is the heart and core of my faith. Besides that witness to others, these ashes may also remind us of our Lord's great love, love so great that He suffered and died on the cross as full and final payment for our sins. That cross also calls for a response from us, a response of love for our Lord.

That is the "treasure of the heart" to which we are called. St. Paul says it this way in today's Epistle: "Be reconciled to God" (2 Cor 5:20), learn to love Him as He loves you. Do not "receive the grace of God in vain" (2 Cor 6:1). And now from that treasure come others: treasures of the heart that call on us to trust His will, direction, and purpose for our lives; treasures of the heart that point us to the fullness of His love for others, a love that moves us to love even the unlovable.

All of this is possible because Jesus died for us and rose again, fulfilling what He Himself called "the sign of Jonah" (Lk 11:29; see also Mt 12:39), a sign the people of Jesus' day had difficulty believing and one that many today still refuse to believe. Thus Jesus adds, "The men of Nineveh will rise up at the judgment with this generation and condemn it, for they repented at the preaching of Jonah, and behold, something greater than Jonah is here" (Mt 12:41; Lk 11:32).

THE STORY OF JONAH

By the power of the Spirit through the Word, we can learn much from Jonah this Ash Wednesday as we learn what it means to store up "treasures of the heart."

Jonah was an eighth-century BC prophet of the Lord. He lived in Israel's Northern Kingdom during the reign of Jeroboam II, son of Jehoash, an evil king, whom the Lord still used to extend the Northern Kingdom as never before experienced. This expansion was "according to the word of the LORD, the God of Israel, which He spoke by His servant Jonah the son of Amittai, the prophet, who was from Gath-hepher" (2 Ki 14:25).

Jonah knew God's love and mercy, as well as His anger over sin. He knew, as he himself writes, that God is "a gracious God and merciful, slow to anger and abounding in steadfast love, and relenting from disaster" (Jonah 4:2). And so, when the Lord called on Jonah to "go to Nineveh, that great city, and call out against it, for their evil has come up before Me" (Jonah 1:2), Jonah ran the other way! But God stopped him.

Finding himself in the belly of a great fish, Jonah prayed, "I called out to the LORD, out of my distress, and He answered me. . . . When my life was fainting away, I remembered the LORD, and my prayer came to You, into Your holy temple. Those who pay regard to vain idols forsake their hope of steadfast love. But I with the voice of thanksgiving will sacrifice to You; what I have vowed I will pay. Salvation belongs to the LORD!" (Jonah 2:2, 7–9). And he was saved.

Vomited onto dry land, Jonah finally went to Nineveh as the Lord desired. There he preached to that large and wicked city a word of Law, "Yet forty days, and Nineveh shall be overthrown!" (Jonah 3:4). After three days Jonah's worst fears were realized: "The people of Nineveh believed God. They called for a fast and put on sackcloth . . . and sat in ashes" (vv. 5–6). "When God saw what they did, how they turned from their evil way, God relented of the disaster that He had said He would do to them, and He did not do it" (v. 10).

JONAH'S RESPONSE TO GOD'S MERCY

Jonah's response was displeasure and anger, the kind of anger and displeasure we might feel if others aren't punished as we think they ought to be, for example, if we have been offended and want the offender to be disciplined. Or it is our response to a hurtful word, to being cut off in traffic, or to see someone else get the favor that we expect.

"Jonah," the Bible tells us, "went out of the city and sat to the east of the city and made a booth for himself there. He sat under it in the shade, till he should see what would become of the city" (4:5). He was there for the show—fire and brimstone, wind and rain, calamity and destruction. Jonah wanted fireworks, but God provided forgiveness and calm, fatherly love and acceptance.

When Jonah learned that day the truth of Joel's word that the Lord "relents over disaster" (Joel 2:13), he became even more angry.

Jonah became so angry, in fact, that he said to God, "I do well to be angry, angry enough to die" (4:9). But God didn't let it happen, and His last word to Jonah is also His word to us today: "Should not I pity Nineveh, that great city, in which there are more than 120,000 persons who do not know their right hand from their left, and also much cattle?" (4:11). Like little children, the Ninevites needed God's fatherly compassion, a compassion that His love, demonstrated to us in Christ's death and resurrection, now calls forth from us—a true treasure of the heart.

Our Response to God's Mercy

As we begin the Lenten season and look forward to our celebration of the fulfillment of the "sign of Jonah," we, like Jonah, need to understand the fullness of God's love and mercy, about which the prophet Joel declares, " 'Even now,' declares the LORD, 'return to Me with all your heart, with fasting, with weeping, and with mourning; and rend your hearts and not your garments.' Return to the LORD, your God, for He is gracious and merciful, slow to anger, and abounding in steadfast love" (Joel 2:12–13).

That love and mercy of our Lord enables us to reach out to others and share with them the salvation from our God, saying to them what the apostle Paul says to us, "Be reconciled to God. For our sake He made Him to be sin who knew no sin, so that in Him we might become the righteousness of God. . . . Now is the day of salvation" (2 Cor 5:20–21; 6:2). By ourselves, we aren't able to do that. We are like Jonah, angry and displeased with all the sin we see around us. We are people who want to declare God's judgment on the world of sin and then wait for the wrath of God to be shown upon them.

But the "show" has already taken place. Jesus died, the curtain in the temple was torn from top to bottom, Satan fell from heaven, his head was crushed, and we won!

And now comes the calm—the calm of the resurrection, the peace that passes understanding. Now comes God's love and mercy to a world of sin and His call to us to "Lay up for yourselves treasures in heaven. . . . Where your treasure is, there your heart will be also" (Mt 6:20–21).

The ashes of Ash Wednesday are a witness, a witness to our faith, and as such, a witness to God's love and mercy for the world. The ashes of this day remind us of the psalmist's prayer to the Lord, "You have turned for me my mourning into dancing; You have loosed my sackcloth and clothed me with gladness" (Ps 30:11).

Earlier in this service we prayed, "Create in me a clean heart, O God, and renew a right spirit within me. Cast me not away from Your presence, and take not Your Holy Spirit from me. Restore to me the joy of Your salvation, and uphold me with a willing spirit" (Ps 51:10–12). That prayer has been answered through the Holy Spirit bringing us to faith in the first place and continuing to lead us forward in faith. As we confess our own helplessness and sinfulness before our God, we discover something truly surprising. The treasures of the heart that Christ invites us to store up have been stored up for us. We don't have to look somber or disfigure our faces because "now is the favorable time; behold, now is the day of salvation" (2 Cor 6:2). We are not alone! God is with us!

"Blow the trumpet in Zion; consecrate a fast; call a solemn assembly; gather the people. Consecrate the congregation; assemble the elders; gather the children, even nursing infants" (Joel 2:15–16)! "For," as Jesus says to us, "where your treasure is, there your heart will be also" (Mt 6:21). The treasures of the heart that we need and desire are ours, now, because of Jesus, by the power of His Spirit.

Rev. David W. Wollenburg

Clothing That Makes the Man

2 Corinthians 5:20b–6:2

THE EMPEROR'S NEW CLOTHES

Many years ago there lived an emperor known for his high opinion of himself. But this did not distress his subjects in the least. After all, the land enjoyed peace, and the rulers of the neighboring countries knew better than to wage war. Travel was safe. Business was good. The people were prosperous. And everybody was happy. The emperor had every reason to be proud of his imperial skill. He also had lots of free time, was very handsome, and well aware of his good looks. His clothes were made to measure and immaculately appropriate for the occasion. In fact, clothes were the emperor's greatest passion, and money didn't matter when it came to hiring the best of designers. The emperor liked to look at himself in the mirror, thinking how the prosperity of his land reflected the greatness of his mind and how the elegance of his clothes showed the sophistication of his taste.

One day two men came to the royal city. They said they were weavers and could manufacture the finest cloth imaginable. Not only was its color exquisite and unlike anything found even in far-off lands, but all clothes made of that cloth possessed the quality of being invisible to anybody who was stupid. Needless to say, the material was difficult to make and, therefore, rather expensive. "Here is something worthy of my greatness," thought the emperor. "Ordinary clothes are for ordinary people, for lazy people, for those who haven't achieved anything in life. But my accomplishments are known far and wide. Look at the prosperity and peace that my people enjoy. I deserve something special." At once he had the weavers begin their work, without regard to cost.

After countless delays and with the imperial bank account nearly empty, the emperor's new suit was at last ready just in time for an important national holiday. Early in the morning the emperor hastened to the weavers' room, opened the door and swayed as his knees gave way. If it hadn't been for one of the servants, he would have collapsed on the floor unconscious. He saw the empty loom, a few odd pieces of furniture, and the two weavers, holding something he couldn't see. "No one can ever know that I'm stupid," thought the emperor. He undressed slowly and the weavers helped him put on his new robes. The parade was to start in less than an hour.

As usual, the procession would go through all the major streets of the capital. This time the turnout was particularly huge, for everyone wanted to see the wonderful new clothes, whose amazing quality was already known.

Besides, the emperor had long been the model to imitate, as far as fashion was concerned. The beginning proved quite promising—all who saw the emperor seemed quite in awe of his new robes. "What exquisite colors! How well it fits him!" they marveled. Cheers of praise and adoration seemed to have no end. And then came the moment of truth. "But he has nothing on at all," exclaimed a little child. "The emperor's naked!" The stunned crowd froze.

Coveting Godhood

So ends Hans Christian Andersen's tale of "The Emperor's New Clothes," in which two swindlers make a fortune on human vanity and overblown sense of self-worth. As we observe Ash Wednesday, this familiar tale offers an insight into human nature that cannot be overlooked.

Recall life in the Garden of Eden. Adam and Eve were made to live in a loving relationship with God and to reflect His love for them in their own relationship and in their stewardship of creation. Theirs was the divine blessing to "be fruitful and multiply and fill the earth and subdue it" (Gen 1:28). In a word, their very being was defined by the love that had brought them into existence and given them a place of honor as stewards over the earth.

Then sin crept into God's creation. Hearing the serpent's deceitful promise that they, too, could be like God, Adam and Eve abandoned their privileged position among God's creatures. By coveting godhood, they separated themselves from the life-giving love of God that had made them and defined them. Their hope was that with the knowledge of good and evil, they would be able to establish their place within creation without anybody's help, without owing anything to anyone. But the much-craved knowledge of good and evil did not make them any more divine. It only opened their eyes to how evil their abuse of God's love had been. It exposed their nakedness. Yes, they were now free to define themselves, to create their own godhood. But this freedom proved to be an endless struggle to cover their shame—a struggle filled with pain, doubt, and death.

The Pursuit of Self-Definition

Ever since the fall, human life has been marked by this solitary pursuit of self-definition. We live in the age of self-made people. We are judged by how much we've achieved in life, how much we spent on our education, how much we earn, and what kinds of cars and houses and clothes we have. Everything about us is meant to make a statement: "This is what I am; this is what I have made myself to be." Like the emperor of Andersen's tale, we achieve and then dress ourselves up in our achievements for others to see.

To be sure, there is nothing inherently wrong with accomplishments, with the pursuit of knowledge, or spending the money one has earned, as long as accomplishments, money, or knowledge do not become our gods. "This is what I am! This is what I have made myself to be!" can never be our creed. When our achievements turn into a means of self-creation, we fall into the sin of Adam and Eve. This sin deceives us into thinking that we are naked unless we achieve and clothe ourselves with our successes. This sin makes us blind to the fact that all we are and all we have comes from the hand of God, the only and true Creator. This sin severs us from the love of God, which formed us in our mother's womb and still continues to define us.

God's Faithfulness

Although we have stripped ourselves of the love of God in an attempt to achieve godhood by ourselves, He has remained faithful and steadfast in His love for us. He continues to provide us with everything we need to support our life. Our achievements do not just "happen"; our mental capacities and the resources that we use are God's gifts to us. Neither our intelligence nor the world around us is, therefore, a springboard to divinity. Yet if the things we attain are treated as such—against God and as if they are not gifts of His life-giving love—they can bring us only to the point of death. And death shows us our foolishness in clothing ourselves with the things of this world. At death we are left naked. Houses and cars, money and knowledge may offer a temporary sense of security. But their beauty withers, their dependability passes away, and in time everything is left bare. Then it is God who, despite the marveling and adoring crowd, whispers, "You are naked! What have you that I haven't given you? You are naked! Do you think that My gifts can be turned into your gods or make you into one? How foolish! You are naked! You are naked."

Unlike Andersen's tale, our story of vanity and overblown sense of self-worth need not end here. For God's love is true love, which neither withers nor fades. In holy love, God's only Son stripped Himself of His heavenly splendor to rescue us from the deadly compulsion to achieve. He became naked for us to save us from our nakedness, to clothe us with His righteousness, to restore us to our God-given place of honor in creation. As our sermon text puts it, "For our sake [God] made Him to be sin who knew no sin, so that in Him we might become the righteousness of God" (2 Cor 5:21). A great exchange indeed! Our sin for His righteousness. Our nakedness for His garment of salvation. We stand resplendent in robes fit for an emperor because God hung in our place, naked on the cross. This may seem like nothing in the eyes of the world, which time and again foolishly clothes itself with things that do not endure. Yes, God's love may seem weak by the standards of the world's rat race, but it is in this love that we find eternal respite, a place where we belong—deliverance.

The Miracle of Divine Love

As we now stand on the threshold of Lent, we ponder again the miracle of divine love; love that did not shrink from death itself to reconcile us to God. Naked and stripped of His glory, Jesus Christ laid down His life so that we might be created anew. It is His love, not our achievements, that defines us. It is His love that overcame the power of death. This is no ordinary clothing, but the finest to be imagined. Christ's righteousness covers our nakedness—Scripture's euphemism for sin. It protects us when we suffer; it stays with us when we die; it goes with us into glory. Through the love of Christ we are God's own people again, made to live in a loving relationship with Him and to reflect His love for us in our relationships with one another and our stewardship of creation. His is this accomplishment.

May the cross of ash on the forehead be a reminder to all of us that it is not the world that clothes us but the love of our Savior. Ashes symbolize the nakedness of the things of this world and the nakedness of sin. But Christ's love covers us and wields power over death. "Behold, now is the favorable time; behold, now is the day of salvation" (2 Cor 6:2). Now is the time of reconciliation.

Rev. Piotr J. Malysz

Maundy Thursday

Symbols for Servanthood

John 13:2–5

This passage in John 13 may be the strangest anticlimax in the Scriptures. "During supper, when the devil had already put it into the heart of Judas Iscariot, Simon's son, to betray Him, Jesus, knowing that the Father had given all things into His hands, and that He had come from God and was going back to God, rose from supper. He laid aside His outer garments, and"—now this—"taking a towel, tied it around His waist. Then He poured water into a basin and began to wash the disciples' feet and to wipe them with the towel that was wrapped around Him" (vv. 2–5). What an anticlimax! Consider the situation.

Events that would bring Jesus to His terrifying hour of rejection and death were already in motion. And Jesus knew it. The awesome task of rescuing condemned humanity and bringing all people back to God had been entrusted solely to Christ. This responsibility was placed squarely in His hands. And Jesus knew it. Jesus, who alone had come from God, was beginning His journey back to God to sit at His right hand in power and majesty. Jesus was aware of that.

Because He knew, should not this Scripture have ended in a different manner? Might it have concluded by describing how Jesus took His seat at the head of the table and His disciples attended solicitously to Him? Or that Jesus turned aside from His disciples to be alone, so that He could focus His thinking on Himself and His task? Or that Jesus, so cognizant that He was destined for glory, could not condescend to perform this menial task? One would have expected such conclusions. And who would have faulted Jesus if He had reacted in any of those ways?

What we get is something else, however. King of kings and Lord of lords and very God of very God notwithstanding, Jesus assumed the duties of a slave, washed His disciples' feet, and dried them with the towel. Who would have expected that? What an anticlimax!

CHRIST AND THE TOWEL

Of course, Jesus did not consider it an anticlimax. What Jesus did with that towel was wholly in keeping with what He did and said elsewhere—that serving one another is the compelling goal of a Christian's life. Moreover, as far as Jesus was concerned, such an attitude of servanthood is not belittling but is what makes a person great in God's sight. Did not Jesus Himself say, "Whoever would be great among you must be your servant, and whoever would be first among you must be your slave" (Mt 20:26–27)?

Therefore, next to the symbol of the cross, which forever controls the content of the message we proclaim, ought to be the symbol of the towel, which forever reminds us that servanthood is greatness.

I'm not sure I want to accept this symbol of the towel and the compelling goal of service that it represents. I would prefer to be served than to serve. Let someone else wash my smelly feet or, in today's terms, shine my dirty shoes and wash my filthy clothes by hand. Let others run an out-of-the-way errand for a needy neighbor or assume some irritating task that interrupts my busy schedule. Get someone else for that—not me. I have more pressing concerns!

Are you ever like that? If so, then how similar you are to the disciples in your self-concern. Aren't we all like that, like those disciples—who that night, at that sacred meal, as Luke's Gospel informs us—squabbled among themselves about who was the greatest? Who should do the serving and who should be served? Whose accomplishments should be recognized and appreciated most? Who gets the honor for working the hardest? Whose name should be placed at the top of the list? Whose face on camera?

These contentious questions reverberated among the disciples in the Upper Room and still reverberate among us. The one question not raised was "Who should take up the towel and wash the dirty feet?" That was not the question anyone considered or the task for which anyone volunteered. No one did. No one but Jesus. So that night, though the shadow of the cross fell across His path, though He knew one of the disciples was betraying Him, one would deny Him, and all would desert Him, He knelt before them and, like a slave, washed and dried their feet.

Today, Christ asks us to follow His example. He stands before us and invites us, as He did His first disciples centuries ago, to take up a life of servanthood. He asks us to reject popular standards for success and urges us to take the towel and go to work with it. The many and varied servant tasks of life await us. They need not be deeds that get noted in newspapers and applauded by the public. They are likely to be the opposite. They may be menial tasks from which we instinctively turn, but menial tasks we can accept, as did Jesus, without loss of self-respect or sense of personal worth. They can be—they should be—the ordinary, somewhat humdrum duties of life at home, at school, and at the office, tasks that must be routinely performed over and over. However, they lose their humdrum and routine character because they are the deeds on which Christ places His stamp of approval. These servant deeds, said Christ, make a person great.

Doesn't Jesus thereby turn topsy-turvy popular notions of success? The natural talents or personal achievements that attract attention don't make a person great. The purpose of service for which they are employed do. The votes garnered or the degrees conferred or the gifts that glisten in the public's eye don't make success, but the ready towel in the hand does. That is what Christ says counts for greatness.

So Christ asks for people willing to be servants. That's asking for a lot, especially in this day and age. By what authority does He do that? What gives Him the right to lay this claim of servanthood on us?

Because He, Himself, was a servant? Yes, that's partly it. Jesus was no classroom teacher good only at describing how to be a servant. He was our model. "I have given you an example, that you also should do just as I have done to you" (Jn 13:15). His whole life was spent in service. This washing of feet was but one episode of many. Think of His miracles. Why did He perform them? Not to razzle-dazzle people with His power but in response to people's needs and their needs alone. Think of His teaching. Why did He weary Himself with words designed to cut through layers of distorted ideas about God and of unworthy ways that one person treated another? To gather crowds of admirers? Hardly. What did He care about gathering admirers? He raised His voice to convince people of the truths for which He died as the Suffering Servant of God. He didn't preach about service, He practiced it, and by that authority He expects it of us. If He, our Lord and Master, was a servant, how much more should we, His followers, be servants!

Christ and the Cross

However, Jesus' authority is more than that of an example. We need that, but we need more. For He not only took up the towel as a servant, He took up the cross as the Savior. He is not only our pattern for life, He is our power. The power of His cross to energize in us a willingness to follow His example—that is our gravest need.

Think what it would be like to have Christ as our pattern for life, but not as our power. Imagine how it would feel to have Christ as an example and nothing more. We would then be challenged to match His humble, self-sacrificial servanthood with our self-seeking behavior. And that would be like attempting to match the brilliance of the noonday sun with a battery-powered flashlight.

Think what it means to have Christ with the power of His cross. There is cleansing power in His cross. There is forgiving love earned for us on the cross that can wash away the blemishes of our self-concern. It can wipe clean the record that has been marred by our grasping for greatness in ways that lord it over others. It can make us stand proud and tall before God as His forgiven children.

Christ cannot cleanse us like that with a towel. But through the cross He can. He presses the cup of His grace against our lips and has us taste with our tongues and eat in our mouths the bread of life, as He did that first Maundy Thursday night with His disciples. "His blood can make the foulest clean" (*LSB* 528:4), as the hymn writer put it. It can. And it does.

It was said Napoleon believed destroying a man's reputation was the best way to ensure his loyalty. How different with Christ! How completely different! He restored our sullied reputation with forgiving grace and thereby enlists our loyalty to Him and to His example of service.

THE CROSS AND THE TOWEL

We need both symbols as Christians. The cross in one hand, telling us of Christ's saving sacrifice, and the towel in the other, reminding us to be servants. We cannot have one without the other. To accept the cross is to receive the towel. To accept the towel is to confess the need for the cross.

Some will say that being a servant is not a satisfying symbol of success. It isn't, except for those whose standard for success is doing the will of God and whose satisfaction is in the blessing of the Lord.

Rev. Paul A. O. Boecler

The Face of the Lamb

Exodus 12:1–14

Look into the faces of the lambs that night, and you'll see what I mean. Look into the faces of the lambs that would shed their blood to provide a safe haven for their owners. Look into the faces of the lambs that would be roasted over the fire and eaten. Look into their faces, and what do you see?

You behold the innocence of an animal looking back at you, that's what. They don't have a clue about what is being done. Although God chose to use their suffering and death, their blood and their body, it was not something to which they consented or about which they were even consulted.

Yet they did the job. They played their role; they pointed to something else, something bigger than what happened in Egypt that night when the angel of death swept through the land and took the lives of any firstborn not found huddled under their blood.

THE FACE OF THE LAMB OF GOD

Look from the faces of the lambs as they await their slaughter, and look tonight to the face of the Lamb of God who takes away the sin of the world. Look into the face of the Lamb who would shed His blood to provide a safe haven for a sinful world. Look into the face of the Lamb who would be roasted over the fires of hell and even give His body and blood to be eaten. Look into His face, and what do you see?

You see the face of one who knows. You see the face of one who wills. You see not the face of an ignorant, nonconsenting animal, but of a fully cooperative human sacrifice. He said: "No one takes [My life] from Me, but I lay it down of My own accord. I have authority to lay it down, and I have authority to take it up again. This charge I have received from My Father" (Jh 10:18). He said, " 'Now is My soul troubled. And what shall I say? "Father, save Me from this hour"? But for this purpose I have come to this hour. Father, glorify Your name.' Then a voice came from heaven: 'I have glorified it, and I will glorify it again' " (12:27–28). "Now is the judgment of this world; now will the ruler of this world be cast out. And I, when I am lifted up from the earth, will draw all people to Myself" (Jn 12:31–32).

THE PASSOVER LAMB

This is what you see in the eyes of the Lamb of God as He goes forward to meet this night. Gathered in the Upper Room, the disciples wait as the meal is brought to them. Did His eyes leave the roasted lamb once it was carried into the room? Picture meeting reality—type meeting antitype. All that that lamb meant for Israel and more, He had come to be for all people. Roasted it was; roasted He would be. Like the lamb, spitted on a tree over the fires. The fires of hell burned and turned in the flame, and this Lamb of God was found writhing in the pain of it all so that He could be Passover to a doomed world.

His blood would mark each body as His own. His sacrifice alone had the strength to turn away death. His body would be given as food for the faithful that they might partake and be ready to move out of this land of darkness and into their true fatherland, the promised land of heaven. His body and blood was the one and only ticket out of condemnation.

Look into His face that night. It's all etched there, written with clarity. "I know what I am doing, and what I am doing I do for love of you and love of all, that whoever will believe this great love will be delivered from the angel of death forever!"

From the Upper Room, where the picture meets the reality, to the garden and the trial and the hill with its three crosses, where the reality of God's great love for humanity shines in the darkness—from start to finish—when you look into the Lamb's face His message is the same: "All this I choose to do for you, for love of you."

THE LIVING MEMORIAL OF THE EUCHARIST

Tonight we gather as Christians have gathered for century upon century. Tonight we celebrate that as the Lamb of God was about to go forth to His voluntary suffering and death, He instituted a memorial. His memorial took up the Passover and went further. His memorial took up the manna and went further. For His memorial is His Eucharist. Here the Lamb gives His flesh as bread and His blood as wine to His own people. Here the Lamb extends His life to give us life, His forgiveness to wipe away all sins. And tonight His own people look Him in the eyes as we receive these gifts and we see written there: "All this I chose to do for you, for love of you, to forgive you and make you My own."

Before the love we see written in the eyes of this Lamb of God, what can we do but fall to our knees in amazement and let His blood mark our mouth and our bodies, and His body nourish our bodies and our souls, crying out, "Lamb of God, You take away the sin of the world! Have mercy and grant us peace!"

Rev. William C. Weedon

The Blood of the Covenant

Exodus 24:3–11

On Sunday, May 18, 1980, at 8:32 AM, Mount St. Helens in Washington State erupted, sending three cubic kilometers of ash and rock skyrocketing into the air and cascading down the side of the mountain at more than 200 miles per hour. On Mount Adams, 35 miles away, Miss Suzanne Christiansen, an eyewitness to this unimaginable scene, dropped to the ground, awestruck by what she had seen.

National Geographic published a series of photographs of this incredible event. A picture is worth a thousand words, so it is said, and these pictures from *National Geographic* vividly portray how we human beings respond to forces beyond our control; forces that threaten us, overpower us, and make us realize just how small and insignificant we really are. The top of the mountain goes *bang* and disappears behind a thick cloud of smoke and ash, and just like Suzanne Christiansen, we fall to the ground, awestruck by what we have seen.

To Be in the Presence of God

In the Book of Exodus we read:

> On the morning of the third day there were thunders and lightnings and a thick cloud on the mountain and a very loud trumpet blast, so that all the people in the camp trembled. Then Moses brought the people out of the camp to meet God, and they took their stand at the foot of the mountain. Now Mount Sinai was wrapped in smoke because the LORD had descended on it in fire. The smoke of it went up like the smoke of a kiln, and the whole mountain trembled greatly. And as the sound of the trumpet grew louder and louder, Moses spoke, and God answered him in thunder. . . . When all the people saw the thunder and the flashes of lightning and the sound of the trumpet and the mountain smoking, the people were afraid and trembled, and they stood far off and said to Moses, "You speak to us, and we will listen; but do not let God speak to us, lest we die." (Ex 19:16–19; 20:18–19)

This is what it is like to be in the presence of God, when sinful human beings are called to stand before the all-knowing, all-powerful, and awe-inspiring Creator of heaven and earth. He is holy. We are not. The psalmist writes, "Clouds and thick darkness are all around Him; righteousness and justice are the foundation of His throne. Fire goes before Him and burns up His adversaries all around. His lightnings light up the world; the earth sees and trembles. The mountains melt like wax before the LORD, before the Lord of all the earth" (Ps 97:2–5).

"Fire goes before Him. . . . His lightnings light up the world. . . . The mountains melt like wax." Who here could stand before all that? I would rather crawl into a hole and hide. That's how the people of Israel must have felt when they were confronted by the Lord of hosts, for they clearly perceived how different from Him they were. How could they ever approach Him? How can we?

The Blood of the Covenant

In the immediate wake of the September 11, 2001, terrorist attack, there went out an unprecedented call, and an equally unprecedented response, for blood. In a matter of days the American Red Cross received more blood from more blood donors than it needed. People knew that where there is blood, there is life or, at least, the chance for life. That has always been true: blood is viewed as the bearer of life and the prerequisite for the maintenance of life. For that reason, in the Old Testament sacrificial blood was used to show that forgiveness of sins and an ongoing relationship with God came with the cost of a life.

God chose Israel to be His own. He lovingly and graciously led them out of slavery in Egypt. He protected them as they passed through the Red Sea and drowned their Egyptian pursuers in the waves. In our text, the Lord now desired to enter into a covenant, that is, into a solemn and binding agreement exclusively with them, in which He would be their God and they would be His people. The terms of this covenant were simple. The Lord would guide, lead, prosper, and protect the people of Israel, and they would do everything that He commanded. To seal this covenant, young bulls were sacrificed and blood was shed. Half of this blood was poured on the altar, symbolizing God's forgiveness of the people and acceptance of their offering, and the other half was sprinkled on the people themselves. This covenantal blood bound them to God in obedience. It was on the basis of blood, therefore, that forgiveness was obtained and a relationship with God was established. The representatives of the people scaled the mountain and ate a fellowship meal together in the presence of the Almighty Himself.

Rebellious Children

The Lord kept the covenant, but the people did not. They abandoned Him and the covenant He made with them for other gods. They adopted the wicked practices of the world around them. They became like rebellious children, unfaithful spouses, straying sheep. Many times the Lord disciplined them, but they refused to repent. Instead of listening to the word of the Lord, they persecuted and killed His messengers. Finally, out of His great love for them, God sent His Son.

The Blood of the New Covenant

A new and better covenant was necessary, which would require a new and better sacrifice.

> Not all the blood of beasts
> On Jewish altars slain
> Could give the guilty conscience peace
> Or wash away the stain.

> But Christ, the heav'nly Lamb,
> Takes all our sins away;
> A sacrifice of nobler name
> And richer blood than they (*LSB* 431:1–2)

We are no better than the people of Israel. We also have behaved like rebellious children, unfaithful spouses, and straying sheep. How often have we known the Lord's expectations of us, but instead of doing His will, we disobeyed. That is no less than sin, and the wages of sin is death. How often have our eyes been dazzled and our gaze been averted by the toys, trinkets, and temptations of this world. In our use of money, for example, have we been faithful to God alone or has the "stuff" of this world come between us and God? That is the sin of unfaithfulness and even idolatry, and the wages of sin is death.

But here is the big surprise: "For while we were still weak, at the right time Christ died for the ungodly. For one will scarcely die for a righteous person— though perhaps for a good person one would dare even to die—but God shows His love for us in that while we were still sinners, Christ died for us" (Rom 5:6–8). Jesus Himself became the sacrifice. Jesus Himself gave His life. Jesus Himself shed His blood for you and for me. "He was wounded for our transgressions; He was crushed for our iniquities; upon Him was the chastisement that brought us peace, and with His stripes we are healed. All we like sheep have gone astray; we have turned every one to His own way; and the LORD has laid on Him the iniquity of us all" (Is 53:5–6).

It sounds too good to be true, doesn't it? How may we be sure of this message? "Drink of it, all of you," Jesus says, "for this is My blood of the covenant, which is poured out for many for the forgiveness of sins" (Mt 26:27–28). Our Savior knows and understands that we are people who live, move, and have our being in a physical world where seeing, hearing, touching, and tasting are all very important to us. So He comes to us in a very real, very physical way.

Imagine what would happen if, as a husband, I daily told my wife that I loved her, but never hugged her, squeezed her hand, put my arm around her shoulder, or gave her a kiss. It wouldn't be long before she would doubt my professed love for her. Why? Most of us need consistent and loving physical contact as a way of ensuring that we are loved. Jesus knows this, and so He comes to us often, meets us personally at the communion rail, and says: "Here I am for you. Eat My body. Drink My blood. I am here for you because I love you. Your sins, they are forgiven. Your faith, it is strengthened. Enjoy the fellowship you have with Me, and when you leave, know that My peace is with you."

Fear not. The blood of the new covenant has been shed for you. So, come up to the mountain. Your Lord and Savior is waiting, and He is anxious and eager for you to be in His presence and eat and drink again.

Rev. William G. Utech

It's the LORD'S Supper

1 Corinthians 11:24–25

Celebrating the Lord's Supper is not an option. It is the Savior's will. He instituted it. He commanded it. He said, "Do this." This night gets its name, "Maundy Thursday," from the Latin word *mandatum*, "command." In the Upper Room, Jesus said, "A new commandment I give to you, that you love one another" (Jn 13:34). It's the night of our Lord's commands: "Love"; "Do this."

The Sacrament of the Lord's Supper is Jesus' gift to His Church. He wants us to extend our hand to receive it. We disrespect Him, our Lord and Savior, when we turn away from His gift of love. It's kind of like going to Grandma's house for Thanksgiving dinner. If we don't show up, she is sure to ask us why we weren't there: "I prepared the meal for you, but you didn't come." It's Grandma's meal, prepared just for us, and we turned away from it.

The big reason we go for Grandma's meal, though, is not that we don't want to offend her. We want to go. The food is great. In the same way, we want to come to our Lord's Supper because the food is great.

Jesus said, "Do this." He commands us to come so that He can serve us. Only if we come can He serve. We call our hour in the Lord's house a "worship service" for just this reason. During this hour, He wants to serve us with this Sacrament to forgive our sin and hold us close in His love. He wants to build us up in His Spirit and send us on our way rejoicing, refreshed, and renewed in His grace.

For me as a pastor, it is a great comfort when the Sacrament is offered at the worship service. I know my sermon may not reach everyone's needs. I know people's minds may wander from the hymns and prayers and readings. But when the Sacrament is served, it is the Lord Himself who comes directly through the bread and wine. No human failing, including the preacher's, gets in the way of Jesus' special, personal touch. This is His moment with us, and we treasure it.

Jesus takes His Supper very seriously, and He asks us to take it seriously as well. Tonight we observe the night when He was betrayed, the night on which our Lord instituted His Supper for all time. We are gathered primarily to receive this Supper in His name. "Do this," He says, and we come obediently and expectantly.

When we accept His invitation, we acknowledge that His gift of love is precious to us. If we ignore it, we reveal what place He has in our lives. Other things are more important. We don't feel a need for His gift. We don't believe it's as important as He thinks it is.

I tell the young people in the First Communion class that the Sacrament is like getting a birthday party invitation from your best friend. What would that friend think if you ignored it? It's his or her party, and you don't care. Or it's like getting an invitation to a meal from the governor or the president. Would you make room in your schedule for such an opportunity? What would he or she think if you just didn't care?

The wonderful thing about our Lord is that He never stops inviting. He never stops offering. He never remembers past snubs. He just rejoices that the lost sheep is back in the fold, safe in His arms.

When we come, we proclaim to all our family members and friends and fellow church members that we want our Lord's love and forgiveness. We leave home, and our neighbors see us. We perhaps talk about this experience at work and even at parties. As St. Paul goes on to say, "For as often as you eat this bread and drink the cup, you proclaim the Lord's death until He comes" (1 Cor 11:26).

What a privilege! What a joy! How we rejoice when each new child in our family or in our church family can join us in the blessing. How we rejoice when each unchurched friend eventually hears the Lord's call and comes to His Table. Our heart leaps for joy as our Lord's does when He sees His beloved children gather for His meal. It is an awesome moment.

Our Approach to the Altar Reflects These Attitudes

At the start of the service, we acknowledge our sins. We also have a brief moment of silence to examine our life. Now the climactic moment is coming when we actually receive the Savior's grace into our bodies and souls. We stand, and our heart starts beating a bit faster. We will soon be at His Table, in His presence, receiving His gift. We approach the Lord's Supper reverently and expectantly. As the ushers come down the aisle, we stop singing as they near our pew. We take a moment to pray. We walk up and respectfully exchange a bow with the officiant. We are bowing together to our gracious Lord. We are in His presence, gratefully acknowledging Him who in grace has called us to His feast.

We extend our hand and receive the bread and the wine, the very body and blood of our Lord. We remember that His body was broken and His blood was shed in payment for our sins. We are washed clean, from the inside out. We are renewed and strengthened by His love. We revel in this moment.

The pastor says words of dismissal. Some people cross themselves, recalling the other Sacrament, our Baptism, when we first received that sign and seal. We smile. We return to our pew and pray our thanksgiving. This is the moment we prepared for. We savor it.

It is the Lord's Supper. We rejoice. Our Lord rejoices.

Rev. Herbert E. Hoefer

The Best Meal You've Ever Had

Luke 22:7–20

What's the best meal you've ever had? I can think of several great meals. There is the Italian restaurant where my wife and I go for Sunday brunch—all-you-can-eat pasta bar, eggs, sausage, and even roast beef, fish, and chicken. I remember family meals on Sunday evening when I was a young boy growing up in Chicago. We sat on the kitchen floor and ate simple sandwiches while listening to the radio together as a family.

What criteria make a meal "the best" you ever had? Is it the food, the fellowship, the price? Tonight, may I suggest, you will be served one of the best meals you ever had because it is a life-giving, life-renewing, life-changing meal that you can have over and over again.

THE NEW COVENANT

Recall that Passover was the significant family meal in the covenant between God and His people. The Israelites were initially slaves in Egypt, living under the harsh treatment of the Pharaoh. Their cries went to the Lord, the God of Abraham, Isaac, and Jacob, who sent Moses to deliver them. Pharaoh refused to let God's people go free. Pharaoh depended on Egypt's gods to lead the country. By sending plagues that overpowered Egypt's so-called gods, the true God convinced Pharaoh to let God's people go. The final plague brought judgment on Egypt's god of life, Osiris or Ptah, as the almighty God sent the destroying angel throughout the land, killing the firstborn in each home. God directed His people to hold a special meal centered on a lamb, whose blood was smeared on the door frame. When the destroyer saw the blood, he passed over the house. The people were protected by the blood of the lamb as a substitute for their lives. As a result of this catastrophic judgment on Egypt, Pharaoh let God's people go. The Israelites celebrated the Passover meal thereafter.

In our text Jesus gathers with His disciples in the Upper Room to celebrate the Passover meal. Jesus was ready for His exodus or departure. During the meal, "He took bread, and when He had given thanks, He broke it and gave it to them, saying, 'This is My body, which is given for you. Do this in remembrance of Me.' And likewise the cup after they had eaten, saying, 'This cup that is poured out for you is the new covenant in My blood'" (Lk 22:19–20). Matthew adds "for the forgiveness of sins" (Mt 26:28).

Jesus instituted a new Passover based on His self-sacrifice as the Passover Lamb. He ends the first covenant and establishes the new covenant promised for the new era. Just as the lamb's blood served as a substitution for the death of the firstborn, so now Jesus' blood substitutes for our death. We are set free from our bondage to sin, to malice, and to evil through the forgiveness He earned by taking judgment into His own body. Sin "lets us go," that is, releases its stranglehold on us. We are free. We are rescued from death and given the certain hope of heaven.

Yes, Jesus "institute[s] a Passover or Supper for you [and me]. [We] shall enjoy it not only once a year, just upon this evening, but often, when and where [we] will, according to everyone's opportunity and necessity, bound to no place or appointed time" (Large Catechism V 47; *Concordia*, p. 437). We will eat a life-giving, life-changing Meal tonight and every time we celebrate the new Passover.

A man was telling a friend that every time he and his wife argue, she gets "historical."

The friend interrupted and said, "Oh, you mean hysterical."

"No," he responded, "I mean historical. She always brings in the past and holds it against me."

In this new Passover meal God does not get "historical." He forgives and forgets our past, as far as the east is from the west. Your sins are forgiven in this Meal.

UNITE WITH JESUS

Sadly, and to their detriment, many Christians neglect this Meal. But for those hungering and thirsting for righteousness, this is a Meal of great benefit. Those who struggle with the old sinful nature, who need strength to handle broken relationships, and who seek the wisdom to make decisions are united with Christ through this Meal.

When a person receives the bread and wine in Holy Communion, that person receives Jesus. As He said, "This is My body." The heart of faith grasps the Word, which puts in the benefit, and then takes out the benefit, namely, all that Christ is according to His Word. The mouth eats physically for the heart and the heart eats spiritually what the body eats physically, and thus both are saved and satisfied by one and the same food.[6]

This special Meal, through which Jesus gives us Himself, changes us into Himself through faith. "To give a crude illustration of what takes place in this eating, it is as if a wolf were to devour a sheep and the sheep were a food so strong that it changed the wolf and turned him into a sheep. Thus when we eat Christ's flesh

---

6 Adapted from Ewald M. Plass, comp., *What Luther Says* (St. Louis: Concordia, 1959), 818.

bodily and spiritually, the food is so strong that it changes us into itself and out of carnal, sinful, mortal men makes spiritual, holy, immortal men. Indeed, we are this already—but, of course, in a hidden manner, in faith and hope; and the fact is not yet evident."[7] This will be evident when the Lord returns and gives us resurrected spiritual bodies equipped to live forever in the new heavens and earth.

This Meal—a life-giving, life-renewing, life-changing Meal—is the best meal we will ever have because we are united with Christ Jesus in this Sacrament. God changes us through the power of the Word, but also in this Meal He gives us His compassion, joy, peace, patience, kindness, moral goodness, sense of responsibility, humility, and self-control—all of which are life-giving, life-renewing, and life-changing. Fantastic!

UNITE WITH EACH OTHER

Consider for a moment grains and grapes as a symbol of Christian fellowship.

> For bread is made out of many grains, ground and mixed together. Out of the many bodies of grain comes one loaf of bread. In it the individual grain loses its body and form and assumes the common body of bread. Likewise, the drops of wine lose their own form and become the body of one wine. Just so should and will it be with us if we use this Sacrament aright.

> Through the love of Christ we are to be changed and are to make the infirmities of all other Christians our own, take upon ourselves their form and needs, and let them have all the good we are able to give them that they may enjoy it. This is the real fellowship and the true significance of this Sacrament. In this way we are changed into one another and are brought into fellowship with one another by love. Without love no such transformation can take place.[8]

Through this Meal, our relationships with one another—our brothers and sisters who kneel beside us—are transformed. There are people who have offended us, or whom we have offended, yet Christ unites us to care for each other, share with each other, help each other. Love comes from Him and overpowers my attitudes. I am changed by this Meal in my relationships and dealings with fellow Christians.

Through this Meal our Lord fashions a fellowship that goes deeper and rises higher than any of human design. "This fellowship consists in this, that all the spiritual possessions of Christ and his saints are shared with and become the common property of him who receives this sacrament. Again all sufferings and sins also become common property; and thus love engenders love in return and [mutual

---

7   Plass, *What Luther Says*, 818.

8   Plass, *What Luther Says*, 814.

love] unites."[9] When Jesus says, "Do this in remembrance of Me," it is as though He were saying, "I am the Head, I will be the first to give himself for you. I will make your suffering and misfortune my own and will bear it for you, so that you in your turn may do the same for me and for one another, allowing all things to be common property, in me, and with me."[10]

Didn't Jesus pray for us to be one in the High Priestly Prayer: "Just as You, Father, are in Me, and I in You, that they also may be in Us, so that the world may believe that You have sent Me" (Jn 17:21)? Nothing harms the witness of the Church more than a Church in conflict. Yet in this feast of love we are united in our witness to this truth: the Father sent His Son to return us to Himself as one fellowship.

Rev. Raymond L. Schiefelbein

---

9 AE 35:51.

10 AE 35:55.

Good Friday

Never Forsaken!

Matthew 27:46

Virtually every word Jesus spoke from the cross until the very end was a word on behalf of someone else. He thought of others first. He looked at His persecutors and asked for their forgiveness. He looked at the malefactor to His right and promised Him salvation. He looked at His mother and gave her a son. As He lived, so He died.

But on the cross, in that moment of confusion and despair, Jesus turned in upon Himself. He looked up into the blackened sky and uttered His bitter lament, "My God, My God, why have You forsaken Me?" (Mt 27:46). None of us can get inside the mind of Jesus and understand the full significance of these mysterious words, but let's try. Perhaps these words will enable us to renew our own sense of intimacy with God the Father.

What must it have been like, this God-forsakenness—who can describe this feeling? Some of us, thinking of past or present experiences, might say, "Surely the worst part must have been inward—the mental, emotional, spiritual anguish. Physical pain cannot account for His cry. Mental torture—is there anything worse than that?"

That's how many of us would answer. We have, at times, felt that God abandoned us—when crushing misfortune crossed our path with its untold heartache and bereavement, or when bewildering disappointment necessitated a drastic change in life's plans, or when we heard no answers to our prayers and no answers to our questions. Then, there was darkness in our world, and hopelessness made a misery of each endless day. In these crises of life, no one knows, no one understands, no one cares. We wonder whether even God cares. We are sure of it—not even God!

So there are days when Christ's cry becomes our cry, and we are sure God has deserted us. But we know there are times when we have deserted God and abandoned His will for our lives. We could have stood by a friend in need, but we decided instead to protect our own interests and passed by our neighbor on the other side. We could have held tightly to God's promise to help us, but we gave in to fear and anxiety. We could have resolved to remain faithful to some noble and Christlike cause, but we caved in to the temptations of the crowd. We could have been bolder in our witness to Christ, but we held our tongue instead and let slip an opportunity to confess the name of Jesus. And just then, when we saw Christ look at us more in pity than in anger, we felt like falling to our knees and saying to Him, as Peter did, "Depart from me, for I am a sinful man, O Lord" (Lk 5:8).

However, some of us take Peter's words too far. We never fully accept forgiveness. We never completely erase bad memories. Wounds caused by wrongdoing are kept open and permitted to fester. God's grace seems too good to be true.

Does God ever slam the door in the face of the penitent? No, but we have hours when a sense of guilt lingers on and on. The merciful Father seems distant and remote. We may even feel like the Roman centurion who responded to Christ's offer to come and heal his servant with the words, "Lord, do not trouble Yourself, for I am not worthy to have You come under my roof" (Lk 7:6).

THE HUMAN JESUS

"My God, why have You forsaken Me?" These words caused difficulty for the Early Church when theologians attempted to formulate the relationship between the divine nature and the human nature of Christ. They might present difficulty for our thinking as well. If Jesus is uniquely and fully divine—"God of God, Light of Light, very God of very God," as we confess in the Nicene Creed—how could Jesus say this? How can God the Son say the Father has forsaken Him? These so very human words of Jesus tend to be an embarrassment for anyone who asserts the divinity of Jesus and His unique oneness with His Father.

However, whatever difficulty these words present in trying to understand the divinity of Jesus, they present no difficulty whatsoever in confessing the humanity of Jesus. Here in these words of confusion and doubt and despair, Jesus demonstrates that He is human. Here He identifies Himself with humanity—with our humanity. Do we feel lonely and friendless? So did Jesus. Have we experienced sorrow and adversity? So did He. Do we wonder about the future and how things will turn out? So did He. Do we question God and demand to know why? "My God, why have You forsaken me?"

This Jesus of ours is human. "Nobody knows the trouble I've seen; nobody knows, but Jesus." That is true not because Jesus is divine, all-knowing God, but because He is human—bone of our bone, flesh of our flesh—with the marks of the crucifixion still on His resurrected body.

THE SYMPATHETIC JESUS

When life's troubles come, and we are tempted to believe that God cannot know what it is like, we need to remind ourselves of these words from Hebrews. The writer refers to Jesus as the Son of God but then writes that Jesus is not "unable to sympathize with our weaknesses, but one who in every respect has been tempted as we are, yet without sin. Let us then with confidence draw near to the throne of grace, that we may receive mercy and find grace to help in time of need" (Heb 4:15–16).

As God, Jesus immersed Himself in our humanity and knew every bit, and more, of what we know: loneliness, sorrow, doubt, despair. God does know what it is like. He does care. We need to remind ourselves that as God, Christ was one with us in our human sin and iniquity. He bore not only our human griefs but also our human sin. He knew not only our times of trouble but also our feeling of separation from God because of sin—our sin, not His. "For our sake He made Him to be sin who knew no sin, so that in Him we might become the righteousness of God" (2 Cor 5:21).

We do experience guilt when we are ashamed of what we have done. Our conscience is soiled, and we cannot rid ourselves of the smell of our sin. But worse, we feel God has driven us out of His garden and locked the gate behind us so we cannot know again the intimate fellowship of a loving father. "My God, why have You forsaken me?"

The Saving Jesus

He hasn't forsaken us; of course He hasn't. He wants us to know the gate to His garden is open, and our past can be left behind at the entrance. He waits within for a friendly and fatherly visit. We don't know this because He appointed a committee to carry out His plans for our reunion or because He issued a written invitation from a distant heaven. God dealt with our sin in a more radical way. We know this because on the cross, in Jesus' body, God bore our sin—the shame of it, the guilt of it, the memory of it.

We, like sheep, have gone astray, but God has laid the iniquity of us all on Jesus. God need do no more than that to cancel what separates us from Him. There is no other deed needed than Christ's crucifixion and resurrection for us to know that we are not alone, God-forsaken in our sin. Not just in Bethlehem's manger but on Calvary's cross, the Word became flesh and dwelt and died among us, full of grace and truth.

During the Civil War, Abraham Lincoln said, "I have not suffered by the South. I have suffered with the South. Their pain has been my pain. Their loss has been my loss." What a noble sentiment! But Lincoln wasn't the South. He did the best he could; he felt with the South—its pain, its loss. But he wasn't the South in person. His land was not ravaged, his home not destroyed, his blood not shed.

But Jesus went beyond sympathetic association with another's loss. We would still believe Him had He said, "I can imagine what it must be like to feel forsaken. I'm trying to put Myself in your shoes. Be assured that you have My heartfelt sympathy and understanding." But how that pales in comparison to what He actually said and experienced in person, "My God, why have You forsaken Me?"

Aren't we glad that Jesus experienced that? Because of that I know, and so do you, that we live through no days darker than those He lived through. We know there is no sinful stain on our record that Christ's blood is not strong enough to remove. He shared our humanity in His life and on the cross. We share His victory now and forever.

Rev. Paul A. O. Boecler

Death Up Close

Isaiah 53:3–12; John 19:28–30

Good Friday and Easter are the climax of our Church Year. As we journeyed through Lent, our eyes looked toward Calvary. Now is the time to stand at the foot of the cross and look up. The mood is somber; the color of the day is black. Yet as we see with eyes of faith, we realize this is a time of victory. Our Lord Jesus experienced death for us that we may share in His triumph over death. Our focus this evening is on these words of the prophet Isaiah. "Surely He has borne our griefs and carried our sorrows" (Is 53:4).

I was 12 or 13. I had certainly *known of* people who had died, but I had not *known* people who had died. Now I was standing beside the casket of my grandfather. I was remembering his smile, remembering him working at his desk in the den, remembering . . . just remembering. Now I had experienced death up close. Death had invaded my life, and death brought hurt. Now I had to deal with pain that was real—I didn't know that I could feel like this. I felt attacked by death. I wasn't sure how to react, where to go, when to talk, what to do. I didn't know what my world would be like without him. As I stood there, trying to make sense of it all, my Aunt Hildy came over and put her arm around me. I don't remember what she said. I do remember that I was glad she was there. I was dealing with death up close, and I was glad to have her near me.

On Good Friday we deal with death up close. We stand not beside a casket of a parent, grandparent, child, or another family member; we stand at the foot of the cross of Jesus Christ. We experience the reality of death, His death. We realize that death does come close—to each of us. Death is an enemy. It would be cold and dark and empty, except that Jesus has come close to us and has faced death for us. His death changes our experience of death. Now we stand before His cross and feel the impact of His love for us as He experienced death up close.

We are not immune to death. To live in our world means that we must face it. Death can be frightening. Sometimes it invades our lives with blazing speed. Sometimes it is slow and relentless as it stalks its target. Death comes in many ways, but it comes. It doesn't always seem fair. It can surprise and shock. It can pierce like a knife. The sky can be blue, the sunshine bright, the air crisp and clean—and then we receive a phone call with bad news, and darkness descends. To be human is to live life that is fragile. Death does come close to us. And death would indeed leave us terrorized and empty except for what took place one Friday. We call it Good Friday, a Friday when Jesus experienced death up close—for us.

The prophet Isaiah painted a poetic picture of what this Friday would be. He described a Savior, a Suffering Savior, who would stand in our place and experience death up close. For us who are part of fallen humanity, death is justice. It is a verdict that fits the crime. We have disobeyed God and deserve death. But now the Suffering Savior comes near. As Isaiah describes it: "He was despised and rejected by men; a man of sorrows, and acquainted with grief. . . . Surely He has borne our griefs and carried our sorrows. . . . He was wounded for our transgressions; He was crushed for our iniquities. . . . The Lord has laid on Him the iniquity of us all. . . . He was cut off out of the land of the living. . . . They made His grave with the wicked" (vv. 3–6, 8–9). He experienced death up close.

What comfort it is that when we face danger, we have a heavenly Savior who seeks to come near! About three months ago, we celebrated Christmas. We rejoiced that God loved us so much that He was born among us. However, the power of the incarnation is not just that Christ was born to join us in life. He was also born to join us in death. He is no distant God, viewing our world from a heavenly executive palace. He comes to be close to the pain. He comes to walk with us in our sorrow. He comes to carry us in our infirmities. He comes to be near to us in all that causes us heartache. He comes to face it all with us.

Our Suffering Savior knows death up close. He felt the bite of death. He winced at the piercing of the nails. He endured the taunting of the crowd and the unjust accusations. He tasted the thirst of death. He didn't simply view death from a casual distance. He was no simple spectator. He joined Himself to us and absorbed the blows of the hammer that should have been ours. In His death He carried our sorrows. He came to the scene of our guilt. He stretched out His hands to receive our sin. He looked death in the eye. He left nothing undone. He said, "It is finished" (Jn 19:30). All was completed; the obligation paid. He closed the book on our failure. The debt was settled. All was accomplished.

On this Friday we stand at the foot of the cross to view a crucified Jesus. We experience death up close, the death of our Suffering Savior. But something has changed. In fact, because of Jesus, everything is changed. We can look into the eyes of death and see not a conquering villain but an enemy that is conquered. Now we can see through the eyes of faith. We see that this is Good Friday. We have vision that takes us beyond this moment and allows us to look to the empty tomb. Now we can see victory in death. Now we can find hope in sorrow. We have a Suffering Savior who experienced death up close—and overcame it. We have a Lord who is like the mother who swallowed the cough medicine first so that her young son would not be afraid to take it. Our Lord swallowed death. He tasted it for us. Now we can follow Him to life.

Death stalked one woman for months. Her cancer had returned. She fought valiantly, but her strength to rally was gone. Her family and pastor formed a circle around her bed and waited. They were looking death in the eye. They felt the pain. They spoke of events in her life, and they marveled at her bravery. They remembered and they prayed, but mostly they waited. Her husband had reached the point of praying that God would simply take her home. God answered that prayer. Everyone felt the loss. But something else took place in that room that evening. As the family experienced death up close, it also experienced the Lord up close. He was near even in the pain. He was bringing the peace that passes all understanding. That little flock was able to see past the grave to the empty tomb.

We, too, are able to see past Good Friday's moment of grief to our Lord's victory. For we have a Suffering Savior. He also experienced death up close. He won. Because He lives, we shall live. Soon it will be Easter.

Rev. Philip E. Streufert

Submission through Suffering

Hebrews 4:14–16; 5:7–9

What is it that we are gathered here today to celebrate—the death of an innocent man? Is that a cause for celebration—the supreme example of sacrificing justice on the altar of the status quo, killing a man so as not to rock the boat? Is that a cause for celebration? That our Lord knows what we go through because He has tasted the bitterness of suffering and death Himself? Is that all we celebrate today?

There are elements of truth in all of that, but none of those explanations plunges deeply enough to plumb the profound depths of joy with which the Church celebrates this day—a joy she celebrates even with tears in her eyes.

THE MEANING OF THE PASSION

What does this day mean? The reading of the Passion tells the facts, but it is the Epistle that opens our eyes to see what these facts mean. These are the facts: Jesus of Nazareth is nailed to a tree. He suffers and then dies, crying out, "It is finished" (Jn 19:30) Why should that be joy? "He was heard because of His reverence. Although He was a son, He learned obedience through what He suffered. And being made perfect, He became the source of eternal salvation to all who obey Him" (Heb 5:7–9).

"Reverence." If we are to understand what Good Friday meant to Jesus, we have to begin with those words. Jesus is very clear that the events of Good Friday came to Him from His Father. With fear and trembling He received the gifts His Father gave—even the gift of suffering, even the gift of death. As He had prayed in Gethsemane, "Not as I will, but as You will" (Mt 26:39).

SUFFERING TEACHES OBEDIENCE

Although He was the eternal Son of the Father, He learned obedience from what He suffered. And it is obedience that the human race owes to the Father—the obedience of creatures to the Creator, the obedience of children made in the image of the blessed Trinity. And it is this obedience that we have failed to render.

THE WILL OF THE FATHER

But our Lord Jesus came into our flesh so that He might be the man who would be man enough to be a man before the Father, to say to the Father with all His heart, "Your will be done." When the Church looks at Good Friday, she sees Jesus as the perfect man—the one who does the will of His Father. But she does not see Him merely as an example, in this regard, but above all as her God-provided substitute. All the obedience the human race had failed to render to the Father, the Lord Jesus goes forth to render on behalf of all—for you, for me.

And that is how "He became the source of eternal salvation to all who obey Him." Obey Him? Yes, because this is His command to you—that you believe in the One the Father has sent for you, that you trust in the perfect submission He rendered on your behalf. This is the great obedience of the Gospel—that you receive the gift God gives you.

The Joyful Celebration on Good Friday

This, then, is the joy the Church celebrates on Good Friday! We have a High Priest who has brought the perfect offering to His Father. The offering He brings is His own unbroken "yes" to the will of the Father, even when that "yes" brought Him suffering and death. This is what He offers up, and this the Father accepts on behalf of all and for all. The Father showed He accepted it when He raised His Son from the dead.

And as if all that were not enough, our Great High Priest gives us even more joy on this day. He gives us the gift of His submissive relationship to the Father as our very own! Not only is He the offering for our sins, but He also becomes "the new and living way" (Heb 10:20) in which we walk.

This is the gift He gave you in your Baptism! There He surrounded you with His forgiveness and applied the fruits of His sacrifice to your life forever. There He planted you into the joy of a life where everything flows to you as gift from the Father who loves you. This is a way of life where the Father blesses you even through—indeed, especially through—your own Good Fridays, your own times of suffering and the hour of death. You are enabled through the Holy Spirit to pray with joy, "Your will be done," because, baptized into Him, you know that your sins have been completely paid for on the cross of Jesus, that your death has been destroyed in His dying, and that you will pass with your Lord through the gate of death to a joyful resurrection.

Good Friday gifts, indeed! Gifts from the man who lived and died and rose again in perfect submission to the will of His Father to become the source of eternal salvation for you.

Rev. William C. Weedon

Hosea, Preacher of the Cross

Hosea 6:1–6

It is "meet, right and salutary" that the Old Testament lesson appointed for this sacred and solemn day in the Church Year comes from the book of the prophet Hosea. Although Hosea lived and ministered more than seven hundred years before the events of the first Good Friday, both his life and his words point us directly to the cross of Jesus Christ. Peter undoubtedly had Hosea in mind, among others, when he wrote in his first Epistle:

> Concerning this salvation, the prophets who prophesied about the grace that was to be yours searched and inquired carefully, inquiring what person or time the Spirit of Christ in them was indicating when he predicted the sufferings of Christ and the subsequent glories. It was revealed to them that they were serving not themselves but you, in the things that have now been announced to you through those who preached the good news to you by the Holy Spirit sent from heaven. (1 Pet 1:10–12)

Under the Spirit's guidance, Hosea proclaimed with his mouth and displayed in his own life what might be called "the threefold message of the cross." Perhaps more vividly and passionately than any other Old Testament prophet, Hosea shows us:

1. the horror of our sin;
2. the terror of God's wrath; and
3. most important, the wonder and splendor of God's love.

THE HORROR OF OUR SIN

The spiritual condition of the people of Israel in the days of the prophet Hosea is summed up in one sentence in the Book of 2 Kings: "They went after false idols and became false" (17:15). The verse goes on to say: "They followed the nations that were around them, concerning whom the LORD had commanded them that they should not do like them."

Keep in mind that this was the nation that God Himself had chosen "out of all the peoples who are on the face of the earth," the nation He had described as His most "treasured possession" (Deut 7:6). These were the people whom Yahweh had plucked from the cruel grasp of Pharaoh, the people whom He had rescued from the land of Egypt, the house of slavery, and brought to the Promised Land, and on whom the Lord had showered blessing after blessing after gracious blessing.

Yet it is this same nation that is described by the prophet Hosea as "a stubborn heifer" (4:16), as "a wild donkey wandering alone" (8:9), as a withered root that

155

yields "no fruit" (9:16). So shockingly corrupt had the nation of Israel become, so blind to their own sin and unfaithfulness, that the Lord commanded Hosea to do a most shocking thing in the hope of somehow shaking Israel out of its spiritual stupor. The Lord instructed Hosea to marry a prostitute and to be faithful to her and to love her though she would undoubtedly be unfaithful to him. Hosea was to model in his own life, in his own marriage, God's relationship with the nation of Israel: though God was completely faithful to Israel, though He loved His chosen people with all His heart, she refused to be faithful to Him. She continued to run after other gods, other lovers; she persisted in her spiritual adultery without any sense of shame or guilt.

"What shall I do with you, O Ephraim?" says the Lord through the prophet. What shall I do with you, O Judah! Your love is like a morning cloud, like the dew that goes early away" (6:4). "In the house of Israel I have seen a horrible thing," says the Lord. "Ephraim's whoredom is there; Israel is defiled" (6:10).

We are missing the point completely if we read these words of Hosea merely as a description of the spiritual corruption of a group of people who lived a long time ago in some faraway place. These words were written down for all people of all times and places—and also for us who are gathered here today. These words describe our natural spiritual condition. They describe the sinful nature that still lives and lurks in the dark corners of our hearts. Hosea's description of Israel's corruption is also an apt description of the horror and ugliness of our sin, our unfaithfulness, our inborn tendency toward spiritual adultery, and our failure and refusal to "fear, love and trust in God above all things."

St. Paul writes in Romans 3: "What then? Are we Jews any better off? No, not at all. For we have already charged that all, both Jews and Greeks, are under sin, as it is written: 'None is righteous, no, not one; no one understands; no one seeks for God. All have turned aside; together they have become worthless; no one does good, not even one'" (3:10–12).

These words of Paul, like the words of Hosea, show us our need for the cross of Jesus Christ. And what we see there, first, is the horror of our sin. Our sin, not His, drove the nails into His hands and feet and the spear into His side. Our pride, our dishonesty, our faithlessness, our broken promises, our lack of love for God and for our neighbor, our selfishness, our brutality, our hypocrisy—they are the cause of Christ's unspeakable agony. Hymn writer Thomas Kelly put it this way:

> Ye who think of sin but lightly
> Nor suppose the evil great
> Here may view its nature rightly,
> Here its guilt may estimate.
> Mark the sacrifice appointed,
> See who bears the awful load;

'Tis the Word, the Lord's Anointed,
Son of Man and Son of God. (*LSB* 451:3)

THE TERROR OF GOD'S WRATH

By showing us our need for the cross, Hosea confronts us, first, with the awful seriousness of our sin. But he does more than that; he shows us why our sinful condition is such a serious matter. Sin is such a serious matter, says the prophet, because it must be punished by a holy God.

Poll after poll after poll continues to show that the vast majority of Americans believe that there is a God. But what kind of God do Americans believe in? Many appear to believe in a "God" who wouldn't hurt a fly, who always smiles and never gets angry; who ignores our faults but will surely reward all the good things we do; who will take everybody (or almost everybody) to heaven someday but would never even think of sending someone to everlasting condemnation in hell.

Those who share this view of God would be shocked to encounter the picture of the true God as revealed in the Book of Hosea. Hosea's God says of His own chosen people: "[I] will remember their iniquity; [I] will punish their sins" (9:9). Hosea's God says: "Because of the wickedness of their deeds I will drive them out of My house" (9:15). Hosea's God says: "I am to them like a lion; like a leopard I will lurk beside the way. I will fall upon them like a bear robbed of her cubs; I will tear open their breast, and there I will devour them like a lion, as a wild beast would rip them open" (13:7–8). Because of your many sins, says Hosea's God in our text from chapter 6, "I have hewn them by the prophets; I have slain them by the words of My mouth, and My judgment goes forth as the light" (6:5). By confronting God's people with God's wrath and judgment against sin, Hosea again points forward with prophetic insight to the cross of Jesus Christ. On the cross the wrath of God against sin—against our sin—was poured out as never before. On the first Good Friday, the anger of God on account of our sin exploded from heaven with such frightening force that the earth shook and the rocks were split and the sun hid its face (Mt 27:45, 51). The terror of God's wrath caused Jesus Himself to cry out in agony from the cross, "My God, My God, why have You forsaken Me?" (Mt 27:46). But as strange as it may seem, that very cry of Jesus from the cross is our cause for rejoicing on this holy day. In that cry of agony and distress, in that cry of dereliction from the cross, in that cry of seeming despair is our hope and our salvation. On Good Friday God's judgment thundered from heaven against our sin, but it did not thunder against us. On Good Friday God's wrath flashed like lightning on account of our rebellion, but not a hair of our heads was singed. Why? Because on Good Friday God's wrath and judgment fell crushingly on Christ instead of us. "He was wounded for our transgressions; He was crushed for our iniquities; upon Him was the chastisement that brought us peace, and with His stripes we are healed" (Is 53:5).

In 2 Corinthians 5 Paul says that "in Christ God was reconciling the world to Himself, not counting their trespasses against them. . . . For our sake He made Him to be sin who knew no sin, so that in Him we might become the righteousness of God" (5:19, 21). "The wages of sin is death," says Paul in Romans 6, "but the free gift of God is eternal life in Christ Jesus our Lord" (6:23).

THE WONDER OF GOD'S LOVE

Yes, the cross shows us the horror of our sin; yes, the cross confronts us with the terror of God's wrath. But above all, and most important of all, the cross stands as sure proof of the incomparable wonder and splendor of God's love for you and me. On the cross, God punished His own Son instead of punishing us. God allowed His sinless Son to die so that sinners like us might live. God rejected His perfect, obedient Son so that He could accept rebels like us as His own dear children. God made Him who had no sin to be sin for us, so that we might be declared righteous and holy in His sight—not because of anything good in us but because of His grace in Christ alone.

In his prophetic vision of the cross, Hosea also saw this incredible love of God. Yes, Hosea's God is a God of wrath and justice. But through the Son who was to come, God's love overcomes His wrath and His mercy overcomes His judgment. After all that His people have done, after all of their sin and rebellion, Hosea's God says, "How can I give you up, O Ephraim? How can I hand you over, O Israel? . . . My heart recoils within Me; My compassion grows warm and tender. I will not execute My burning anger; I will not again destroy Ephraim; for I am God and not a man, the Holy One in your midst, and I will not come in wrath" (11:8–9).

And so in our text for this Good Friday, the prophet speaks to Israel in words that speak also to us today—to us who know the horror of our sin, who know the terror of God's wrath, which we by our sins have deserved, and who know with even greater certainty God's grace in the cross of Christ.

Through Christ's blood shed for you on Calvary's cross and through the "spring rain" of your Baptism into His death and resurrection, you have been healed, you have been revived, you have been restored, you have been set free to live in God's presence. Press on, then, to acknowledge Him. Press on to acknowledge the Lord and His grace with your lives and with your lips, with your sacrifices of praise and thanksgiving and holy living. Return to the Lord today and every day in true repentance and full confidence in His forgiveness. Return to the Lord, that He may bind up your wounds and send you forth—like Hosea—in His name, with His Word, with His love, to bind up the wounds of others by pointing them to the wounds of Him who suffered and died on Calvary's cross, and who said, "On the third day [I] will rise" (Lk 18:33).

Rev. Joel D. Lehenbauer

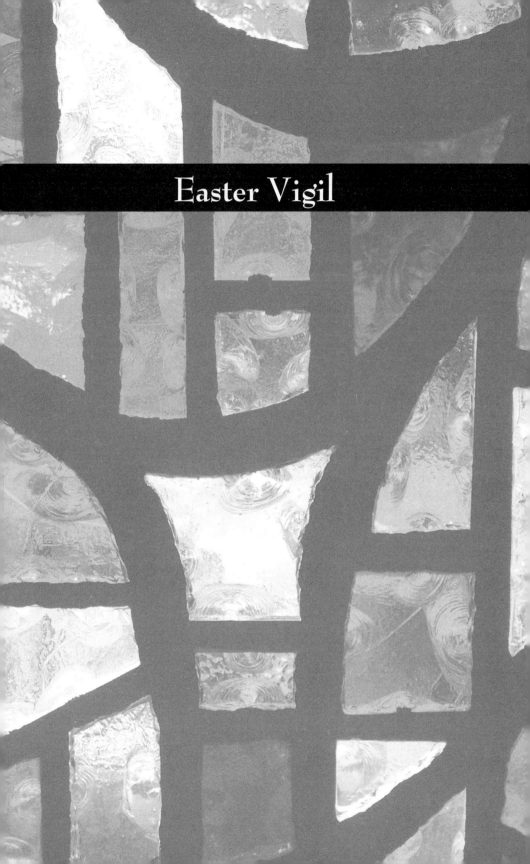

Easter Vigil

With Him through Death

Daniel 3:1–29; 1 Peter 3:17–22; Matthew 27:57–66

Death is a powerful and frightening reality in our human existence that no one can escape. We may be able to cheat it for a while or forestall it with medicine or surgery, but eventually death will have us. It is a curse we carry around in our flesh because of sin. When mankind first rebelled against God, death passed to all humanity. The Lord said to Adam, "In the day that you eat of it you shall surely die" (Gen 2:17). And die Adam did; and not only Adam but all his descendants. The whole of humanity became cursed with death. And now that curse is passed on to us. Although we don't like to face it, we see the marks of death in our flesh: aging, illness, disease, pain. These point the way to that inescapable end that lies ahead of us. Death is powerful and it is frightening.

THE COST OF FAITHFULNESS

Three young men who refused to bow down to the idolatrous image of Nebuchadnezzar faced the grim specter of death one day in Babylon. They were to be thrown into a fiery furnace for their uncompromising faith in the God of Israel, a faith that would not allow them to worship the golden idol of their king. So the king decided to give them one more chance. He would again sound the call to worship so that they might fall down before the golden idol. He warned them, "But if you do not worship, you shall immediately be cast into a burning fiery furnace. And who is the god who will deliver you out of my hands?" (Dan 3:15). The three men responded; "We have no need to answer you in this matter. If this be so, our God whom we serve is able to deliver us from the burning fiery furnace, and He will deliver us out of your hand, O king. But if not, be it known to you, O king, that we will not serve your gods or worship the golden image that you have set up" (3:16–18). Were they not afraid? Could they not see the certainty of their doom? Where did they get such boldness in the face of death?

They were thrown into the furnace and fell down in the midst of the flames. The flames were so hot that the men who escorted them died at the door to the furnace. As the king watched to see Shadrach, Meshach, and Abednego burn, he beheld that the flames were doing them no harm! Moreover, only three men had been cast into the furnace, and now he saw a fourth whom he described as being "like a son of the gods" (3:25).

The men walked through the furnace and back into the land of the living, unscorched, not even smelling of the fire through which they had passed. These men had passed through certain death and had come out alive. In faith they feared not the flames of death but trusted in the Lord their God. As they confessed to Nebuchadnezzar, "Our God whom we serve is able to deliver us" (3:17).

OUR LORD ENTERED INTO DEATH FOR US

This day we recall that our Lord entered into death for us as well. He who is God Almighty entered into our humanity and took the curse of our death upon Himself. On Good Friday the purpose of His incarnation was fulfilled as He was crucified and died upon the tree. Then they laid Him in our tomb and sealed the door.

But death could not contain the Son of God, St. John Chrysostom writes that Christ "annihilated" death, completely turning the tables on Satan. When Christ descended into hell, it was not as a captive but as Victor—and those in hell saw God.[11] So Christ has conquered death. He did not lay in the tomb defeated, but triumphantly awaited the resurrection on Easter morning when His triumph would be proclaimed to the world.

And now He brings that triumph to us through the Sacrament of Holy Baptism. St. Peter says that Baptism now saves us through the resurrection of Christ. He, having died, risen, and ascended is now in authority over all angels, authorities, and powers; even over the power of death itself. He who once entered into the fiery furnace to save the three young men, who spent that Passover in the grave, now enters into the waters of Holy Baptism to bring us through death into life. There, according to St. Peter, we are put to death in the flesh and made alive in the Spirit. That which was sinful in us by the power of God's Word through Baptism is slain and destroyed. And in its place God creates a new man who lives according to the Spirit, who will never die. And so, having died and risen again spiritually, we have nothing to fear from physical death. Its sting is removed and its power is gone. For Christ will also open that sealed tomb, and by His Word will call our bodies forth to eternal life. And so in the face of the fear of our own mortality, in the face of death, we too confess, "Our God whom we serve is able to deliver us." He has removed our fear and destroyed forever the power of death with His own resurrection. To Him be glory with the Father and the Holy Spirit now and forever.

Rev. David A. Kind

---

11 J. Robert Wright, *Readings for the Daily Office from the Early Church* (New York: Church Hymnal Company, 1991),174–75.

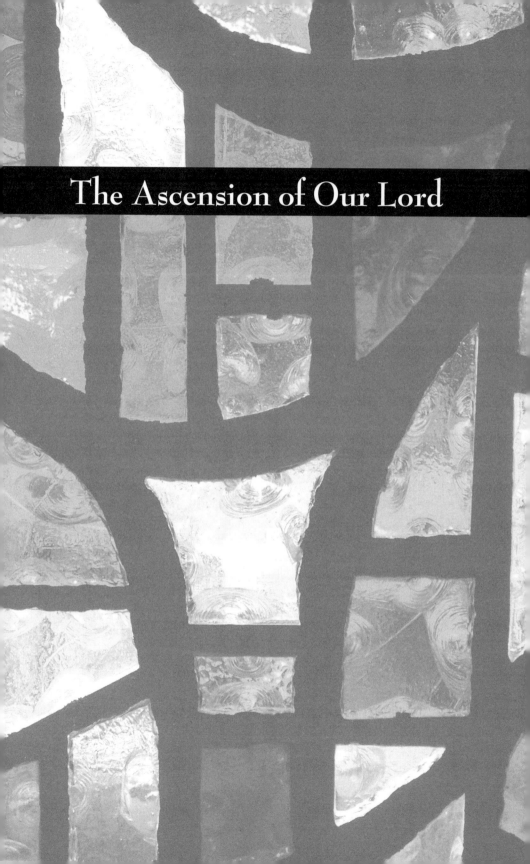

The Ascension of Our Lord

The Blessing
of Jesus' Ascension

Luke 24:44–53

Jesus' Death Opened the Way
to His Ascension to Glory

Jesus had talked about this homecoming more than once. After the Passover meal was ended (the last Passover He would eat with them this side of eternity), He said, "I came from the Father and have come into the world, and now I am leaving the world and going to the Father" (Jn 16:28). The disciples heard these enigmatic words and all too quickly responded, "Now You are speaking plainly and not using figurative speech! Now we know that You know all things and do not need anyone to question You; this is why we believe that You came from God" (Jn 16:29–30).

It was a response that didn't quite fit. Jesus challenged them, looking deeply into their souls. "Do you now believe?" (Jn 16:31). Perhaps He said this because He knew the troubles that lay ahead for them. Of course they did yet not understand (or believe?) that His departure would be by way of the cross. "This shall never happen to You" (Mt 16:22), shouted Peter when Jesus foretold such a death. And when it did come on that awe-full Friday afternoon, the sight and experience scattered and shattered them. Of the chosen disciples, only John was at the foot of the cross, standing next to Mary who would become his mother. Those two and just a few heartbroken, but faithful, women.

Perhaps the words Jesus had spoken, "I am leaving the world and going to the Father" (Jn 16:28), were lost from their memory by now—and one could hardly fault them for that. But they were the words of Jesus, and they were true to eternity. At the moment He cried from cross, "Father, into Your hands I commit My spirit!" (Lk 23:46), He left this world. He was indeed going back to His Father! The profound mission He had come to accomplish at the will and beckoning of His Father was complete. He was ready to go home.

Jesus Returns to Heaven a Different Man

What a homecoming it would be for Jesus! In His great and almost final prayer (John 17), our Lord Jesus had earlier said, "Father, glorify Me in Your own presence with the glory that I had with You before the world existed" (v. 5). Although we could never plumb the depth of their meaning, these words point to the power and dignity, the honor and glory that belonged to this pre-incarnate One when He reigned with the Father and the Spirit before time began! Now, at this ascension event, Jesus is going back to this glory! He is going home!

But things have changed for Jesus! He returns as a different man. As He entered earth, Jesus had "made Himself nothing, taking the form of a servant, being born in the likeness of men. And being found in human form, He humbled Himself by becoming obedient to the point of death, even death on a cross" (Phil 2:7–8).

He Takes His (and Our) Humanity with Him

Some surmise that when Jesus returned to heaven and the right hand of the Father, He eschewed His humanity and "cleansed" Himself from all that. But not so. Wonder of wonder, this Jesus, who is both divine and human, takes His full humanity with Him to heaven's glory. It is true to say that one of us has made it all the way to the right hand of the Father because we are united with Him in every way! St. Paul sings of the unity we have with the glorified Lord through these words to the Romans, to the people of Colosse, and thus to us.

> If we have been united with Him in a death like His, we shall certainly be united with Him in a resurrection like His. . . . Now if we have died with Christ, we believe that we will also live with Him. (Rom 6:5, 8)

Through the miracle of Baptism, we are forever united to our Lord Jesus. In this unity with Him, we also ascend to the right hand of the Father!

> If then you have been raised with Christ, seek the things that are above, where Christ is, seated at the right hand of God. Set your minds on things that are above, not on things that are on earth. For you have died, and your life is hidden with Christ in God. When Christ who is your life appears, then you also will appear with Him in glory. (Col 3:1–4)

And if that were not sufficient, we have these words from St. Paul to the Ephesians:

> I do not cease to give thanks for you, remembering you in my prayers, that the God of our Lord Jesus Christ, the Father of glory, may give you a spirit of wisdom and of revelation in the knowledge of Him, having the eyes of your hearts enlightened, that you may know what is the hope to which He has called you, what are the riches of His glorious inheritance in the saints, and what is the immeasurable greatness of His power toward us who believe, according to the working of His great might that He worked in Christ when He raised Him from the dead and seated Him at His right hand in the heavenly places, far above all rule and authority and power and dominion, and above every name that is named, not only in this age but also in the one to come. And He put all things under His feet and gave Him as head over all

things to the church, which is His body, the fullness of Him who fills all in all. (Eph 1:16–23)

One Day We Will Be There with Him in Glory

Because we are united forever to Jesus and all that He did, so in a mysterious and wonderful way we have ascended with Him. We comprehend this now through faith, but in that age to come we will experience it fully. We will be with Him in glory! Jesus prayed for this: "Father, I desire that they also, whom You have given Me, may be with Me where I am, to see My glory that You have given Me because You loved Me before the foundation of the world" (Jn 17:24). The Father answers His Son's prayer! Thanks be to God!

Luke records the ascension of Jesus: "Then He led them out as far as Bethany, and lifting up His hands He blessed them. While He blessed them, He parted from them and was carried up into heaven" (Lk 24:50–51). How wonderful to know that as Jesus was taking His earthly presence from us, He did so with a blessing on His lips. "While He blessed them," Luke says. I wonder what that blessing is? Not was. *Is!*

I am comforted to remember other blessings and promises He gave: "In My Father's house are many rooms. If it were not so, would I have told you that I go to prepare a place for you? And if I go and prepare a place for you, I will come again and will take you to Myself, that where I am you may be also" (Jn 14:2–3). Yet another promise: "And behold, I am with you always, to the end of the age" (Mt 28:20). And another: "Surely I am coming soon" (Rev 22:20).

The Lord's ascension! A blessing for Jesus and also for us!

Rev. Thomas R. Zehnder

We've Got Mail

Acts 1:1–11

One of the few movies I've enjoyed in the past few years is *You've Got Mail*, starring Tom Hanks and Meg Ryan. In this movie Tom Hanks plays an owner of a huge bookstore chain that opens a new store in New York City, just a block or so away from a small, family-owned children's bookstore, run by the character played by Meg Ryan. The two then become heated competitors, and by the end of the movie the small children's bookstore has to close its doors.

In the course of the movie, the two bookstore owners meet each other in a chat room on the Internet, not knowing each other's identity. Soon they begin communicating with each other using electronic mail. In time they become wrapped up in their e-mail romance. At the end of the workday each rushes home to turn on the computer—hoping that when they go online they will hear the words "You've got mail." If they do, they know they have a message from the other.

E-mail has become a convenient way to keep in contact with family and friends. When my wife or I turn on our computer and go online, more often than not we like seeing the notification that "we've got mail" and anticipate what the message might be and who sent it.

A MESSAGE FROM OUR LORD

What if our ascended Lord Jesus sent us e-mail? What if we logged on, read "You've got mail," then discovered the message was from Jesus? What if He sent us e-mail—to tell us some good news, to say that He's coming to be with us, to ask us to do something for Him, to send us an invitation, or just to tell us that He's watching over us and caring for us? That would be exciting!

Not by that means, of course, yet Jesus does send us a message. Instead of using a computer, He uses God's Word. Throughout the pages of Holy Scripture, He tells us the Good News of His salvation for us. In that Word He tells us that He comes to be with us and to be a part of our lives. There He calls us to be His servants and disciples. There He invites us to worship Him in His house. There He tells us that He is watching over us and is most certainly caring for us. The message is as real as a message we receive from a friend through e-mail or even regular mail. And unlike in the movie *You've Got Mail*, we aren't left guessing who's on the other end.

Just as people nowadays use e-mail to send messages to their family and friends, Jesus uses the Word to send a message to us, His people. His message

167

comes to us again and again as time after time we "log on" to God's Word and Jesus is on the other end. In the first chapter of Acts, Jesus sends an important message to His apostles and to all of us as well. In effect, Jesus is telling us, "You've got mail. You've got mail from Me."

You Will Be My Powerful Witnesses

So what is this message Jesus has sent us? Jesus concludes His words in Acts 1 with this important message: "You will receive power when the Holy Spirit has come upon you, and you will be My witnesses" (Acts 1:8). This message goes out to us and to all of Christ's Church here on earth.

Sometimes, however, those statements—"You will receive power" and "You will be My witnesses"—may cause us some discomfort. Together, in essence, Jesus is telling us, "You will be My powerful witnesses." Personally, I would not describe myself in this way. In the Bible there are powerful witnesses such as Peter and Paul and the other apostles. In our present day there are powerful witnesses such as Billy Graham and "The Lutheran Hour." But it's difficult for us to imagine ourselves in their shoes. We're just "regular" church members, doing the best we can in our lives and in our congregation. Others may be powerful witnesses for Jesus, but for the most part we would not include ourselves in that list.

We Can't Make Ourselves into Powerful Witnesses

Notice that when we think or talk like that, we seem to be looking for ways or doing things to make ourselves into powerful witnesses for Jesus. And if we do think that way, we'll never be sure if we've done enough to reach that level. Then the next question becomes "Have I done enough for Jesus, period? Have I done enough powerful things for Him?" If we think this way, we'll never be sure if we've done enough or been powerful enough to please Him. And if we're not sure about that, can we be sure of being acceptable in the sight of our ascended, glorified Lord to live eternally with Him in heaven?

If we are honest with ourselves, we know that of ourselves we are less than Jesus' powerful witnesses—much less. We confess it in our liturgy: "I, a poor, miserable sinner." All that we are and all that we do as sinful human beings fall completely short of fulfilling Jesus' call to be powerful witnesses. But the good news is this: we don't have to make ourselves powerful witnesses.

If we read and follow God's Word rather than following our own thinking, we'll give up on trying to make ourselves powerful witnesses. We didn't send Jesus e-mail one day saying, "God, I want to be a powerful worker in Your Church. I want to stop being a failure, and I want to start serving You. From now on I will be Your witness."

Jesus Does the Work to Make Us His Witnesses

Instead, it is Jesus who sends each of us this message: I've made you My witness despite who you are. I've taken care of it for you. While you were still powerless in your sins and failures to be My witnesses, I died for you (Rom 5:6–8). At the cross I was crucified in weakness. Yet by God's power I live (2 Cor 13:4), and because I live, you will live eternally with Me in glory (Jn 14:19). As your risen and ascended Lord, I have given you power to live for Me—to be My witness in this world. And as you witness for Me in your life, I will be with you always (Mt 28:20).

The power to be Christ's witnesses is not something we produce or manufacture. It can't be. If we think it is, we'll never be able to see ourselves as the witnesses that our ascended Lord calls us to be. But when our Lord Jesus does the work, through the power of the Holy Spirit, we are exactly what He says we are.

We "Forward" the Good News to Others

One of the great things about e-mail is the ease of forwarding a message that you have received to as many people as you would like, so that others may read it and benefit from it as well.

God is the source of the Good News of salvation. He is the source of the message that we have been forgiven and given eternal life through the cross and empty tomb of Jesus Christ. Through the power of His Word and Sacraments He has sent that message to each of us, personally. And by the power of the Holy Spirit He enables us to forward that message to other people. He enables us to forward the message of Jesus Christ to those who need to hear it—those who are sick, those who are hurting, those who are lonely, those who are troubled. God also enables us to forward the message of Jesus Christ to those who haven't heard it or who are skeptical about it. Whether supporting mission efforts with our dollars or sharing the message of Christ with someone who doubts the power of God in his life, we have a powerful message to forward. The work of saving people is God's work. Yet God has made each of us and given each of us the means to forward and spread that message both near and far.

Today and every day our ascended Lord is telling each of us, "You've got mail." And in that mail—which is God's Word, which is our Baptism, which is the Lord's Supper—He tells us again and again that the weaknesses of our sin and our failures to be His witnesses have been nailed to the cross. That's a great message to get, because by ourselves we'd never be able to be His witnesses. But because Jesus has called us to be His witnesses, that's exactly what we are. And because He has given us power through the Holy Spirit, that's exactly what we have.

Rev. Gregory S. Michel